Puzzling Portraits

Puzzling Portraits

Seeing the Old Testament's Confusing Characters as Ethical Models

A. J. CULP

Foreword by
M. DANIEL CARROLL R.

WIPF & STOCK · Eugene, Oregon

PUZZLING PORTRAITS
Seeing the Old Testament's Confusing Characters as Ethical Models

Copyright © 2013 A. J. Culp. All rights reserved. Except for brief quotations in critical publications or reviews, no part of this book may be reproduced in any manner without prior written permission from the publisher. Write: Permissions, Wipf and Stock Publishers, 199 W. 8th Ave., Suite 3, Eugene, OR 97401.

Wipf & Stock
An Imprint of Wipf and Stock Publishers
199 W. 8th Ave., Suite 3
Eugene, OR 97401

www.wipfandstock.com

ISBN 13: 978-1-61097-588-9

Manufactured in the U.S.A.

Scripture quotations are the author's translation, unless otherwise indicated.

Scripture quotations marked (NIV) are taken from the Holy Bible, New International Version®, NIV®. Copyright ©1973, 1978, 1984, 2011 by Biblica, Inc.™ Used by permission of Zondervan. All rights reserved worldwide.

For my parents:

In memory of my mother, Dianne Culp:
    who lived humbly and gently and who loved her family fiercely

And for my father, Jeff Culp:
    from whom I learned the virtues of discipline, wisdom, and hard work, and that to say something simply and clearly is to say it well

Contents

Foreword by M. Daniel Carroll R. • ix
Preface • xiii
Acknowledgments • xv
Introduction • xvii

1   The Landscape of Old Testament Ethics • 1
2   The Role and Significance of Narrative • 13
3   The Use of Individual Stories • 27
4   Theme and Characterization • 36
5   Judges 7:15—8:33: An Exegetical Study • 56
6   The Ethics of Judges 7:15—8:33 • 102
7   Conclusions • 114

Bibliography • 119

Foreword

WE LIVE IN TROUBLING times. The economic future of every continent appears tenuous; armed conflict continues apace in several regions of the world, while violence increases in local schools and neighborhoods. Drug trafficking, terrorism, ecological changes, global migration and immigration reform, cultural views of marriage and family, the power and reach of the media—the list of today's ethical issues is long, the topics are complex.

Ideally, the Christian faith should offer a welcomed, thoughtful orientation on these matters, one that is grounded in the principles and wisdom of its Scripture. Indeed, there are those who do investigate what the Bible might have to say, directly or indirectly, about these moral challenges. This quest always has been the stuff of biblical ethics.

At the same time, in some quarters a new set of questions about the nature of the Bible, especially the Old Testament, and its God are being asked. Doubts arise about whether the Bible can offer an acceptable word for modern realities. Critics of the Old Testament and Yahweh argue that both are violent, misogynist, and xenophobic. This mistrust—even rejection—of the Old Testament, in whole or in part, comes from the so-called new atheists, like Richard Dawkins and Christopher Hitchens, but also from those who claim the Christian faith. Even Old Testament scholars from broadly evangelical backgrounds now mistrust large swaths of the Old Testament.[1]

1. See, for instance, Eric A. Seibert, *The Violence of Scripture: Overcoming*

Puzzling Portraits

This disquieting situation vis-à-vis the Old Testament's potential contribution to contemporary life requires a fresh engagement with the biblical text. This new consideration of the Old Testament as a source for ethics begins with the conviction that it needs *to be read differently*. The Old Testament should be appropriated in a manner commensurate with its function as the holy writ of the church—that is, in its canonical shape with confidence in its relevance.[2]

A. J. Culp's *Puzzling Portraits: Seeing the Old Testament's Confusing Characters as Ethical Models* can play a constructive role in this enterprise precisely at this point. The goal of this volume is to present a method of reading biblical narratives, which examines the literary intricacies of these accounts in order to appreciate better their power as transformative literature. The impact of literature on the moral imagination of readers has been explored by luminaries like Martha Nussbaum, whom Culp cites, but also by others, such as author and Harvard professor Robert Coles.[3] It is in the density of characters' lives and their ethical quandaries that readers find echoes of their own lives and moments of decision. Soundings in literature, in other words, are opportunities for reflecting on a life lived wisely and well.

The opening chapter of *Puzzling Portraits* surveys the publications of important scholars of Old Testament ethics to demonstrate the need for a more full-orbed literary approach. In chapters 2 and 3, Culp utilizes the work of Robin Parry and Gordon Wenham, who show how biblical stories shape ethical thinking and suggest ways for applying virtue ethics to narratives.[4] In chapter 4,

---

the *Old Testament's Troubling Legacy* (Minneapolis: Fortress, 2012); Kenton L. Sparks, *Sacred Word, Broken Word: Biblical Authority and the Dark Side of Scripture* (Grand Rapids: Eerdmans, 2012).

2. See M. Daniel Carroll R., "Ethics and Old Testament Interpretation," in *Hearing the Old Testament: Listening for God's Address*, ed. Craig G. Bartholomew and David J. H. Beldman (Grand Rapids: Eerdmans, 2012), 204–27.

3. Robert Coles, *The Call of Stories: Teaching and the Moral Imagination* (Boston: Houghton Mifflin, 1989); *Handing One Another Along: Literature and Social Reflection* (New York: Random House, 2010).

4. Both continue to explore the ethical significance of the Old Testament.

Foreword

several who work in Old Testament narrative, particularly Robert Alter and Meir Sternberg, serve as the sources for explaining characterization. This literary feature is the focus of the ethical reading of the Gideon account that occupies the final two chapters of the book. That narrative in Judges 7–8 is a case study for analyzing the dynamics of vice and virtue within a covenant relationship. Gideon's faithlessness results in the loss of blessing for himself and the people.

In *Puzzling Portraits*, Culp adds solid research to continuing efforts to validate the abiding significance of the Old Testament canon for ethics.[5] As the supervisor of the thesis that is the basis of this publication, it gives me great joy to commend the work of this young scholar to those who desire that the Old Testament remain a light unto their path and a fire in their bones.

M. Daniel Carroll R. (Rodas), PhD
Distinguished Professor of Old Testament
Denver Seminary

See Robin A. Parry and Heath A. Thomas, eds. *Great Is Thy Faithfulness? Reading Lamentations as Sacred Scripture* (Eugene, OR: Pickwick, 2011); Gordon H. Wenham, *Psalms as Torah: Reading Biblical Song Ethically*, Studies in Theological Interpretation (Grand Rapids: Baker Academic, 2012).

5. For example, Matthew R. Schlimm, *From Fratricide to Forgiveness: The Language and Ethics of Anger in Genesis*, Siphrut 7 (Winona Lake, IN: Eisenbrauns, 2011); cf. Richard S. Briggs, *The Virtuous Reader: Old Testament Narrative and Interpretive Virtue*, Studies in Theological Interpretation (Grand Rapids: Baker Academic, 2010).

Preface

The content of this book originally appeared as my MA thesis, submitted to Denver Seminary in May of 2007. As such, its substance and scope reflect that nature. Scholarly readers may at various points wonder to themselves things such as, "But what about such and such a view?" or "Couldn't this be further nuanced?" The answer in most cases is, yes, the work could be further strengthened and nuanced. I am well aware of this and, someday, may undertake the task of remedying it. For now, however, I am convinced that the book as it stands still offers a genuine contribution to scholarship. After all, its guiding question of how to understand the Bible's complicated characters as ethical models is an old and persistent interpretive tangle, ever in need of a fresh approach.

Acknowledgments

This work owes much of its existence to the labors of Drs. Richard Hess and M. Daniel Carroll R. In addition to their oversight of an excellent Old Testament program in general, in which I learned the skills and tools of biblical scholarship, these two men served as my thesis readers in particular. Their engagement with what initially must have been rather rough pieces of thinking has contributed to the final product in invaluable ways. Danny in particular has shaped my processes of thinking and writing and my approaches to Scripture, especially evident in the present work's literary and ethical concerns. It is no exaggeration, then, to say that whatever the virtue of the present work, it is certain to have suffered without Rick and Danny.

Last but not least, I wish to thank the good people of Wipf & Stock, who have kindly agreed to publish this work. May their model of publishing—which emphasizes merit over salability—serve the community well.

Introduction

In the world of literature a complex character is a virtue, for it shows humanity as it truly is: a mixture of magnificence and wretchedness. In the realm of moral writing, however, a complex character is a vice, for it leaves things gray rather than drawing lines between black and white behavior. So what happens when literature combines both, when it gives a moral message but does so through complicated characters? How then does the reader know what behavior is bad or good, what to eschew or embody? For readers of Old Testament narrative, this is precisely the problem. But what makes the dilemma worse is that these stories are, for most readers, not just instructional tales but authoritative Scripture. So the question becomes doubly important: How should readers draw ethics from the conflicted lives of Old Testament characters? That is the question this study seeks to address.

Now, such a question naturally involves two larger disciplines in biblical studies: the poetics and ethics of narrative. Poetics illumines the way in which Old Testament narrative speaks, ethics the unique content and texture of its morality. To consider these only alongside each other, however, would lead us marginally closer to an answer. Instead, we must investigate them more narrowly: namely, by finding and analyzing the exact point at which poetics and ethics overlap. That point, we suggest, is character portrayal. The Old Testament's portrayal of characters holds the key to unlocking their ethical meaning. Methodologically, then, we seek to answer the central question—how to draw ethics from complex characters—by examining the way in which Old Testament narrative portrays its characters.

Chapter 1 begins this quest by considering the state of scholarship on Old Testament ethics, with a particular concern for the place of narrative. The hope is to locate our own question about complex characters within the larger landscape of scholarship. We attempt to do so by analyzing the views of four scholars that represent a fair spectrum: Walter Kaiser, John Rogerson, Christopher Wright, and Waldemar Janzen. What is found, though, is that while each has unique emphases and ideas about ethics, none has an entirely satisfying position on the role of narrative in general and individual stories in particular. As such, the question with which the chapter closes is this: What is the role and significance of narrative in Old Testament ethics?

Chapter 2 seeks to answer that question. Its discussion turns around three central scholars: Robin Parry, John Barton, and Gordon Wenham. Parry's idea is that biblical narrative serves a much larger role in ethics than is normally attributed to it. Using Barton's models of ethics—imitation of God, natural law, and God's declared will—Parry shows how narrative is a necessary element of each model, which together form the whole of Old Testament ethics. He goes on to argue that beyond being a constituent element of ethics, narrative also contributes uniquely to it. Wenham, then, forwards a foundational idea: biblical law reveals the floor of moral living and narrative the ceiling. That is, unlike much common opinion, it is not law but narrative that reveals the ideals of the Old Testament. The law simply shows the point at which one's morality was too bad and needed to be punished; the narrative actually fleshes out the ideals of moral living.

Having found that narrative is in fact central to Old Testament ethics, in chapter 3 we look at how this translates into individual narratives. That is, we consider how to understand the ethical message of a particular story. The works of Wenham and Parry again prove invaluable. Wenham suggests a general structure for approaching stories, which has three parts: virtue ethics, virtue criteria, and rhetorical criticism. The first part, virtue ethics,

Introduction

offers a way in which to approach narrative ethically, a way that focuses on virtue, practical wisdom, and the good life. The second part, virtue criteria, offers parameters by which to confirm the presence of commended virtues in the text. And the third part, rhetorical criticism, seeks to understand the particular elements of stories. Here Parry's method is found particularly helpful, for it suggests more specific ways in which to approach individual narratives. However, it is argued that still there remains a need for better tools, ones more attuned to the study of character portrayal in ethics.

Chapter 4, then, seeks to locate such tools. It does so by dialoguing with two major scholars in the poetics of biblical narrative, Robert Alter and Meir Sternberg. From Alter and Sternberg, it becomes clear that in order to understand complex characters, two literary tools are especially needed: theme and characterization. Together these help establish the proper framework for understanding characters. Theme, on the one hand, is important in that it establishes a center point between the many story elements; it shows the point at which the pieces meet. Characterization, on the other hand, is crucial in how it both identifies particular narrative features and distinguishes their significance. Thus, theme and characterization allow us to interpret characters sensitive to their literary context.

With the theoretical framework established, chapter 5 moves to a particular text: Judges 7:15—8:33. The point is to exegete the passage in order to locate its own message within the movement of the larger book. To accomplish this, we engage two scholars at length: Robert O'Connell and Yairah Amit. But while each offers a good and helpful study on Judges, neither is entirely satisfying. So we use a variety of other scholars to flesh out our understanding of the book of Judges and the Gideon account. From these, we find that Judges primarily is not about kingship. Rather, the message regards the corruption of Israel due to its covenant unfaithfulness. Gideon plays a central role in the corruption in that he is first among the judges to commit idolatry, tribal brutality, and sinful foreign liaisons. What is more, his story acts as a pivot for the book: from Gideon onward, the judges and the nation grow increasingly worse.

Chapter 6, then, is the culmination of the study. It seeks to integrate the theoretical and exegetical findings into the ethical interpretation of Judges 7:15—8:33. What we argue here is that a negative book like Judges requires a slightly different ethical approach. Instead of looking for virtue, one has to look for vice. This notion arises from the Aristotelian view that vice is the corruption of virtue. And so the way in which each vice corrupts its corresponding virtue is shown through the way in which each character fails to live the good life. Thus, we extract specific vices and analyze them in regard to how they detract from the good life. We conclude, then, by discussing how Gideon failed to live the good life—that is, how his own vices kept him from living a life befitting one of Yahweh's leaders.

1

The Landscape of Old Testament Ethics

Old Testament ethics is an area of study that has many diverse opinions, so to truly do it justice would require a work larger than this one. At the same time, however, it is necessary to establish at least some boundaries and locate this study within them. This will be done by summarizing and discussing four major views that fairly represent a certain spectrum of Old Testament ethics.[1] The central idea of this spectrum is that the Old Testament is of enduring ethical value. Each of the four views has its own ideas as to the particulars. Therefore, to outline the shape of the views, summaries will be constructed around three major issues: basic method, locus of study, and what each sees as the bridge between ancient and modern values. Because the larger study centers on narrative, we will note how each of the four views sees narrative fitting in. It will become clear that although some of the approaches forward good ideas regarding narrative, none is entirely satisfactory, and the issue must be considered more fully.

---

1. It has been noted that "Old Testament ethics" has three related but separate meanings: descriptive, prescriptive, or evaluative ethics. In this case, not dealt with are those approaches that see Old Testament ethics strictly as a descriptive venture. On the three meanings, see Wright, "Ethics," 259.

Puzzling Portraits

WALTER KAISER

In the world of Old Testament ethics, Walter Kaiser's approach is one of the simplest.[2] Its goal is to uncover enduring ideals and apply them to contemporary situations. The place where he finds these ideals is the express commands of God. The way in which he suggests to bridge Old Testament and Christian ethics is by extracting principles from the texts and reapplying them to modern situations. Of course, such simplicity has brought on a host of critics, some fair and others not. What should be noted, however, is that Kaiser's system is not simple for the sake of simplicity. It is simple because Kaiser believes this is the theological solution.[3] That is to say, for him the biblical idea of humanity is one of damaged intellect, reason, and conscience. Accordingly, humanity cannot be left to its own devices when it comes to ethical choices, but instead must be directed clearly, which is why God issued direct commands to the people of Israel. Thus to use the Old Testament ethically, one must look at God's express commands to humanity, extract their principles, and apply them to our current situations.

The locus of Kaiser's approach is in the express commands of the Old Testament, mostly in the Pentateuch, but also in the wisdom and prophetic literature.[4] Concerning those found in the legal material of the Pentateuch, Kaiser follows the traditional model of dividing laws into three categories: moral, civil, and ceremonial. Accordingly, he sees only the moral ones as being binding on Christians, not the civil or ceremonial (which were fulfilled in Christ). These commands of God are the primary witness to ethical ideals in the Old Testament.

According to Kaiser, the bridge between Old Testament and Christian ethics is through a process of isolating and extracting principles. Here he draws from the ideas of John Goldingay, in which principles can be extracted from legal texts. Basically, this method looks at a specific command, draws out its underlying

---

2. Kaiser, *Toward Old Testament Ethics*.
3. Ibid., 5.
4. Ibid., 42.

general principle, and then works to apply it to a specific contemporary situation by using what he calls the "ladder of abstraction."[5] Therefore, the way in which one can overcome the particularity of Old Testament law and use its essence for contemporary application is by locating and extracting principles.

In summary, Kaiser's approach focuses on the express commands of God. In practice, this turns out more often than not to be the moral commands of pentateuchal legal texts (rather than, say, the oracles of the prophets). The bridge between the Old Testament ideals and Christians today is the generalizing of principles. By identifying and isolating the general principles underlying the law it is possible to apply them to specific contemporary situations. According to Kaiser's written work, the role of narrative is very limited.[6] However, it should be noted that narrative plays at least two secondary roles.[7] First, it establishes the context of the law. And second, it lays the groundwork for creation theology, by which Kaiser justifies his approach to Old Testament ethics.

JOHN ROGERSON

John Rogerson's views on Old Testament ethics are probably the most sophisticated considered here.[8] For him, the initial step toward biblical ethics is a proper understanding of Scripture's contextual nature. To understand the enduring ideals arising from the text, one must discern how cultural factors have shaped and colored them. Another important element for biblical ethics is the motivation for behaving rightly. What reasons does the Old Testament give for moral action? How do they affect Christians today?

---

5. Kaiser has developed this further in *Toward Rediscovering the Old Testament*, 155–66.

6. Though not articulated clearly in his written work, Kaiser does grant narrative a role in Old Testament ethics, mostly through the extraction of principles. Kaiser discusses this in his courses, which was made clear to me in a personal correspondence with Richard Hess on April 6, 2007.

7. Kaiser himself never says this, but his approach implies it.

8. Rogerson, *Theory and Practice*.

Puzzling Portraits

And the last piece of Rogerson's approach concerns the formal structures that manifest mercy and grace in society. What sorts of these constructs does the Old Testament mention, and how do they serve as examples for contemporary people of faith? Respectively, Rogerson calls these three foundational elements "natural morality," "imperatives of redemption," and "structures of grace."

Natural morality is the idea that in every time in history there has existed between thoughtful people a common idea of right and wrong.[9] However, this moral consensus is not fixed; it changes as people's sensibilities change. The general movement in history has been toward moral progress.[10] These ideas impact Rogerson's views on Old Testament ethics in a couple of significant ways. First, what the Old Testament reflects is not a single unified ethic, but a mosaic of ideals, specific to individual groups in particular contexts. This contrasts the notion that Scripture reveals the comprehensive, unchanging will of God.[11] And two, following the first point, interpreters must adopt methods commensurate with Scripture's nature. Especially important is the study of the ways in which biblical values are similar to or different from those of the surrounding ancient cultures. That type of inquiry illumines the ethical processes employed by Israel to manifest God's unique moral demands in his people's society.

The second element of Rogerson's approach is the imperative of redemption. It is the reason for ethical behavior given by the Old Testament. The basic foundation for the imperative is located in "those parts of the Old Testament where the motive clause of commandments or instructions mentions God's deliverance of Israel from slavery."[12] Israelites were to treat each other with grace and mercy because God had done so with them. This notion has particular reference to how those in power should treat the weak and the poor (Deut 5:13).[13] What is interesting about the imperative of

9. Ibid., 16.
10. Ibid.
11. Ibid., 17.
12. Ibid., 18.
13. Ibid.

The Landscape of Old Testament Ethics

redemption is how it affects natural morality: the former pushes the latter into deeper sensitivity. Rogerson cites Exodus 21:1–11 and Deuteronomy 15:12–18. He says the chronologically later Deuteronomy passage, which deals more generously with the slave woman, shows that the imperative of redemption caused an increase in sensitivity over time.

The final piece of Rogerson's method is the structure of grace. Structures of grace are concrete ways in which God's ideals are lived out institutionally in society. They are meant "to work out graciousness in practical terms, so that both those who administer it and those who benefit are aware of the graciousness implied."[14] The desired effect of these mechanisms is not to give the needy sustenance alone; structures of grace also aim to enable people to become self-sustaining citizens. Rogerson uses Deuteronomy 15 and Leviticus 25 (the Jubilee) as examples. The former addresses the release of slaves, the latter the liquidation of debt and restoration of land. The aim of each is to restore the independence of individuals through practical, quantifiable measures. The locus of Rogerson's study is not in any particular section of the Old Testament. Rather, his work is spread across a variety of texts and genres. Natural morality is found especially in legal (e.g., Exod 21:28–29) and prophetic (e.g., Amos 1:6) material.[15] Imperatives of redemption have at least two locations: law and narrative. Primarily, the imperatives are given in laws that use a motive clause based on God's delivering Israel from Egypt (Exod 21:1—23:19; Deut 24:17–18; Lev 19:34). Because the motive clauses harken back to narrated events (such as the exodus), the imperatives of redemption are grounded in biblical narrative. Structures of grace also are located in law and narrative.[16] The legal material manifests specific applications of ethical constructs in Israelite society (See Deut 15 and Lev 25).[17] The narrative reveals Israel's efforts to implement these structures.

14. Ibid., 25.
15. Ibid., 16–17.
16. Ibid., 24.
17. Ibid., 25.

For Rogerson, the bridge between Old Testament and Christian ethics is found in the interplay of the imperatives of redemption and the structures of grace. It is not that the Old Testament gives precepts for contemporary living. Rather, it offers an example of the process by which the imperatives of redemption led to the structures of grace.[18] This process, in turn, should be used to form Christians' moral thinking and involvement. Though people of faith today should not mimic Israel's moral system, they ought to be guided by the central Old Testament imperative of redemption: to emulate God's deliverance of the oppressed and needy. That deliverance includes physical, economic, and political liberation. Rogerson also asserts that Christians should draw upon imperatives of redemption mentioned in the New Testament, such as in Galatians 3:27–28. The implementation of structures of grace is something to be directed by experts in the fields of economics and sociology.[19] Christians should be involved in the process, but they must consult experts on how best to design and install institutional structures to benefit people.

In summary, John Rogerson holds that the Old Testament is valuable for ethics in at least two ways. First, it illumines the ways in which Israel succeeded and failed to implement and live out morality in society. These serve as examples as to how God's people might apply his desires to culture today. And second, the Old Testament provides a means to understand the unique bent of Israel's ideals in comparison to those of the neighboring peoples. Perhaps most poignant is the notion that Israel was to behave mercifully and graciously because God had acted that way toward Israel. This imperative of redemption should guide Christians also. However, for Christians the primary act of God's redemptive work is not the exodus; it is the crucifixion.

What role does narrative play in Rogerson's approach to ethics? Narrative assumes important roles in both the imperatives of redemption and the structures of grace. Though the imperatives of redemption are made explicit in motive clauses of laws (Exod

---

18. Ibid., 28.
19. Ibid.

21:1–23:19; Deut 24:17–18; Lev 19:34), they are rooted in narrated events. God justifies commands according to the stories of his own action in history. Also, these stories work to refine Israel's natural morality, raising the nation's sensitivities to new heights. And regarding structures of grace, Israel's efforts to incarnate God's desires in society are recorded in narrative. The law dictates moral structures, and the narrative chronicles exactly how it worked out in real life. Therefore, in Rogerson's approach to Old Testament ethics, narrative functions on multiple levels.

CHRISTOPHER WRIGHT

Fundamental to Wright's approach is the idea of a theological framework.[20] That framework helps deal with the problem of the Old Testament's great diversity and size by providing a governing hermeneutical paradigm. Ultimately, this paradigm discerns the unique situation of historical Israel while maintaining the enduring trajectory of God's intentions. There are three elements at the base of this framework: God, Israel, and land, which can also be thought of as the theological, social, and economic angles on the worldview triangle.[21] God serves as the fixed point on the triangle, with his purposes and intensions being constant. Israel and the land, however, serve only as intermediate points. What this means is that Israel and the land are not ends in themselves, but only serve as examples of God's purposes and desires at a particular point in history. Their far-reaching value is that they point to the greater reality of God's desires for all the earth.

The locus of Wright's study is the whole Old Testament story, because viewed through his theological lens, the story itself reveals something of God's enduring ideals for humanity. Unlike other scholars, Wright does not give priority to one part over another, for each is an organic part of the whole. The law, for example, is important only inasmuch as it plays a part in the story. Its significance is

---

20. Wright, *Old Testament*, 17.
21. Ibid., 20.

limited to the role it plays in that narrative and how it fits into the theology of land and society. To give it any more voice is to extend its reach beyond what was intended. Thus in Wright's approach the entire Old Testament is of value, for it is an organic system whose parts cannot be separated from the whole.

The bridge between Old Testament and Christian ethics lies in Israel as paradigm. Wright's idea of paradigm has two senses: broad and narrow.[22] Paradigm in the broad sense refers to a constellation of beliefs and values held by a community. In the narrow sense, it means a concrete model or example of the application of those communal beliefs and values. Regarding Israel, the broad paradigm includes beliefs such as monotheism and Yahweh as king, and the narrow paradigm includes their manifestation, such as laws for the needy (Exod 22:21–27) or a clan-based system of land tenure (Josh 13–21). Each meaning of paradigm is valuable to Old Testament ethics. To use Israel as an ethical paradigm, one must "look for and articulate the principles the paradigm embodies and then see how they can be reconcretized in some other context."[23] Wright offers as an example the Old Testament institution of Jubilee.[24]

Jubilee was an institution that dealt with proclaiming freedom to slaves and restoring land to families (Lev 25). If during the preceding fifty years Israelites had been enslaved due to debt or had sold land to make ends meet, they were to be freed from bondage or given back their land, respectively. The practical goal of Jubilee was to maintain the unique community that God had established. Economically, the institution served to guard against the acquisition of land by a wealthy elite, which would result in oppression and alienation.[25] Land was to remain equitably distributed

22. Ibid., 67–69. Wright here largely follows Thomas Kuhn's two senses of "paradigm." Kuhn was the scholar who broke ground with his ideas on paradigms in the sixties. See Kuhn's *Structure of Scientific Revolutions*.

23. Wright, "Ethics," 70. It should be noted that Wright sees both paradigms and principles as necessary to ethics. Once principles are extracted, the paradigm should not be discarded, lest the system lose its integrity.

24. Ibid., 198–211.

25. Ibid., 207.

The Landscape of Old Testament Ethics

among the people, so as to allow commoners the means to provide for themselves. Contemporary application would strive to create situations to enable similar means of familial provision. Socially, Jubilee aimed to preserve the integrity and dignity of families. It accomplished this not by moral admonishment, but by "legislating specific structural mechanisms to regulate the economic effects of debt."[26] Current practice might consider how to create such mechanisms for the welfare system. Theologically, present in the institution of Jubilee are several tenets of Israelite faith, including God's sovereignty, providence, redemption, and forgiveness. To observe Jubilee was to understand that these qualities characterize God and are meant to manifest in his people.

In summary, Wright's approach makes use of the entire Old Testament. The way he proposes to bridge the gap between Old Testament ideals and Christian ethics is by using Israel paradigmatically. That is, by understanding the overall purposes of God in Israel and by separating these from the culturally unique elements, Christians can use the nation of Israel as an ethical model for Church praxis. What, then, is the place of narrative in his scheme? Beside the metanarrative, which serves as the Old Testament's guiding framework, Wright suggests that individual narratives illumine the kinds of virtues desired for God's community.[27] He seeks to draw an "identikit" portrait of the virtuous person, as conceived by the Old Testament. However, in practice Wright uses very few narratives (Job and 1 Sam 12:2–5).[28] Mostly he focuses on wisdom and prophetic sayings to draw up his constructive portrait.

WALDEMAR JANZEN

Like Wright, Waldemar Janzen holds that the best way to approach Old Testament ethics is by employing a paradigm.[29] However, the

26. Ibid., 208.

27. Ibid., 364. Wright heavily emphasizes that individual ethics have no place apart from their relation to the larger community.

28. Ibid., 371–73.

29. Janzen, *Old Testament*.

Puzzling Portraits

way in which he does this is somewhat different. For Janzen, "paradigm" means a pattern of ideal behavior.[30] In the Old Testament there exists a collection of these patterns. As one reads the text, the paradigms come to form one's mind regarding ethical living. Whereas Wright looks to extract principles from a passage, Janzen argues that principles are necessarily bound to the text and must remain imbedded. Thus the reader learns ethics not from a combination of stories and principles, but from the stories themselves.

Though Janzen acknowledges the value of the entire Old Testament, his approach is anchored by five narratives: Genesis 13, Numbers 25, 1 Samuel 25, 1 Samuel 24, and 1 Kings 21. Each is central to one of five ethical paradigms, respectively: familial, priestly, wisdom, royal, and prophetic.[31] The individual paradigms are portraits of ideal living for the various social roles in Israel: family, priest, sage, king, or prophet. These different paradigms, however, should not be viewed as offering separate or conflicting ideas of ethical living. Rather, each demonstrates Israel's core values in a particular manifestation of life. The familial paradigm overarches the rest; it is the collective idea of what it meant to live as a good Israelite.[32] Though the other four models only applied to specific people, the familial pertained to each and every Israelite. Janzen's idea of paradigm means that characters' behaviors, not characters themselves, are meant to be emulated. To demonstrate particular virtues in particular circumstances is the point of paradigms. Janzen's bridge from Old Testament to Christian ethics is never clearly articulated. One is left to one's own devices to piece together the bridge. Two elements seem most valuable. First, Janzen asserts that principles should not be extracted from stories, because ethics are inseparable from their narratives. And second, he says the concept of ethical living is like that of a "good driver."[33] To be a good driver, one does not memorize a list of rules

---

30. See Wright, "Ethics," 368. Wright uses "paradigm" to refer to the larger structure of Israel, as presented in the Old Testament.

31. Janzen, *Old Testament*, 9–19.

32. Ibid, 2.

33. Ibid., 29.

The Landscape of Old Testament Ethics

or principles, but subconsciously constructs an idea of good driving though stories heard. It may be concluded that for Janzen one learns ethical behavior from reading the paradigmatic stories of the Old Testament and, from those stories, constructing a mental idea of moral living. That mental idea is put into action in ways faithful to the enduring Old Testament ideals and applicable to modern contexts.

In summary, Janzen's approach considers the entire Old Testament, though it centers on five paradigmatic narratives. These narratives model ideal behavior in specific situations. Of the five paradigms, the familial one is chief. It illustrates behavior applicable to all Israelites, regardless of life station. Readers bridge the gap between Old Testament and Christian ethics by absorbing the ideals of the paradigm narratives and living them out in current situations. For Janzen, the place of narrative is large. On the one hand, he sees narrative as epistemologically primary. All other genres—law, oracles, etc.—are framed by narrative. Narrative locates and gives significance to the other forms of writing. On the other hand, narrative offers specific examples of ethical living. Each paradigm is anchored in a specific story, which illustrates righteous behavior in a particular situation. Janzen makes clear, though, that what the biblical author offers for imitation is behavior, not people.

CONCLUSIONS

This chapter has sketched a general picture of some recent studies in Old Testament ethics, and has shown that a great diversity exists in scholarly opinion regarding proper methodology, locus of study, the bridge between Old Testament and Christian ethics, and the role of narrative. Most convincing of the ones considered are the approaches of Wright and Janzen. Two features seem especially valuable. First is the notion that enduring ideals undergird the entire Old Testament. This is significant because it means these canonical writings of old, if approached properly, are still valuable for moral living today. Second are Wright and Janzen's constructive approaches. Instead of limiting their study to one or two genres, as many others do, they both consider the whole counsel of Scripture. Using many genres, both approaches form a governing moral web in which specific passages can be located and interpreted. Nevertheless, there are still some deficiencies in their approaches. On the one hand, Janzen is ambiguous on exactly how Old Testament ideals may be imported into modern lives. Wright's work is helpful here, as he articulates a much clearer way to bridge the gap: by using Israel as a paradigm from which to extract principles and apply them to situations today. And on the other hand, Wright does not deal adequately with the role and significance of narrative. Thus the next chapter will consider in depth the place of narrative in Old Testament ethics.

2

The Role and Significance of Narrative

In the last chapter it was shown that common views on the role of narrative in Old Testament ethics are not entirely satisfactory. Two areas were noted where this is especially evident: the significance of narrative to Old Testament ethics as a whole and the use of individual stories ethically. We take these issues in turn. At the outset, it should be noted that for the present chapter, two ideas are foundational: narrative is necessary to biblical ethics and offers it a unique contribution. These two ideas, however, are not held commonly among scholars. The following discussion provides evidence for them and probes the role of narrative in Old Testament ethics and the proper use of individual stories. The works of Robin Parry and Gordon Wenham serve as important resources.

AN ESSENTIAL ELEMENT

Parry asserts that narrative is the place where Old Testament ethics "lives and moves and has its being."[1] That is to say, ethics is so rooted in the overarching biblical story and its individual stories

---

1. Parry, *Old Testament*, 48.

that one cannot gain a proper understanding of morality apart from them. He sets out to demonstrate this by showing the centrality of stories to the Old Testament models of ethics proposed by John Barton.[2] The reason it is important for Parry to use Barton's models is as follows. Barton's scheme is widely accepted in Old Testament ethics. It provides a strong and reliable foundation for ethical inquiry. However, Barton does not attribute the same value to narrative as Parry does.[3] Therefore, Parry uses Barton's position—a mainstay in the field—to show that the value of stories for Old Testament ethics goes beyond what Barton allows.[4]

2. Barton first wrote on this in "Understanding Old Testament Ethics" and then later modified and expanded on it in "The Basis of Ethics in the Hebrew Bible." Both of these can now be found in his book *Understanding Old Testament Ethics*.

3. See Barton, *Ethics*, 71–74. Barton believes Old Testament narrative does not lend itself to a virtue ethics approach (one that looks to identify and extract virtues). In his view, the closest thing to virtue ethics that biblical stories offer is the illustration of the nature of humanity. This illustration serves as an item of reflection and consideration.

4. At this juncture, another idea should be discussed. Chapter 1 outlined the general ways in which narrative is viewed in regard to biblical ethics. What was not noted, however, is that some scholars deny that Old Testament narrative has any value whatsoever for ethics. A case in point is Cyril Rodd, who makes his position clear: "I conclude that the purpose of the narrators was not primarily ethical. None of the passages effectively raise moral dilemmas, and through them neither God nor the writers offer moral teaching to the reader" (*Glimpses*, 292). His stance appears to be based on three assumptions: (1) that the ethical ideals contained in the text are too distant and different from those of modern culture to understand (286); (2) that the complexity of characters does not allow for clear ethical evaluation (285); and (3) that biblical stories are not historical and therefore do not reveal the true morality of Israel (282–83). Each of the three is a legitimate concern, though each also has reasonable answers. For assumption (3), it should be noted that a variety of scholars disagree with Rodd's view of the nature and historicity of biblical narrative. See the essays of Millard, Long, Younger, Halpern, and Knoppers in *Israel's Past*. Assumptions (1) and (2) are dealt with in this study. A brief discussion suffices for now. Rodd grounds (1) in the false presupposition that the ethics and action of an event "cannot be separated" (284). That is, the underlying principle of an action cannot be extracted for use in other contexts because, at some level, ethics and action are necessarily bound. Concerning (2), it is argued here that complex characters are not fatal to narrative ethics. Rather, the employment of certain rhetorical tools can help handle the multiplicity of character details.

The Role and Significance of Narrative

The basic question that Barton has sought to answer is, why should people act in a certain way? He finds that the Old Testament answers this in three main ways: obedience to the declared will of God; natural law; and imitation of God. "Obedience to the declared will of God" means that people ought to act in a certain way because God commands it. This is perhaps the clearest of his models, for the Old Testament is full of God's direct commands. The legal material is especially noted for using this rationale. "Natural law," as defined by Barton, is the idea that things can be deemed right in proportion to how they align with the created order. Undergirding this is the idea that the workings of the world reflect the ways of the creator God. Therefore, actions that accord with the created order are ethical, and those that do not are unethical.[5] The "imitation of God" model asserts that people should act in a certain way, because God would act in that way. Though only a few biblical texts make this explicit (Exod 20:8-21 and 22:26-7; Lev 19:2), it may actually form the foundation for many other texts.[6] How does Parry believe narrative is related to Barton's models?

Imitation of God

Parry suggests two ways in which narrative is necessary to the imitation of God model.[7] First, the virtuous character of God, which Israel is called to imitate, is known only through acts in history. That is, Israel can only imitate what they have seen acted out. Static qualities may characterize God, but the demonstration of these must take on the form of behavior in history, which is storied in nature. God's mercy is shown in the exodus deliverance,

---

5. Of course, Barton does say that most natural law material has been subsumed under the divine command model.

6. Parry, *Old Testament Story*, 51. Parry uses as an example the fact that Exod 20:8-11 and 23:12 contain the same Sabbath command, though the former is the only one that uses the imitation of God as justification. Thus he suggests that the imitation of God may be so common that it is rarely mentioned explicitly.

7. Ibid., 53.

his justice in the exile, and his loyalty in the return from exile. Second, the imitation of God must take place within the larger story of Israel. It would not make sense outside of that realm. This is because imitation is dependent upon particular behavior in particular circumstances. One must have the specific context in which to situate virtuous behavior. Ultimately, then, the imitation of God is necessarily storied in form: Israel observed the character of God through his actions and sought to live life accordingly.

Natural Law

Story's foundational nature for natural law is found in both obvious and less-than-obvious places. Any biblical notion of natural law is rooted in the creation story. Beginning the entire biblical story is the creation account, which sets out the proper ordering of all creation. God and humans, plants and animals, land and seas all take their place on the scene of life. But in considering the created order, one must also recognize the event and effects of the fall, which twisted and corrupted this natural order. As such, there is a tension between the intended order and that which now exists. In fact, the story of redemption can be understood as the work of God to restore proper relationships in the created order.[8] This idea of creation, therefore, lays the foundation for the whole biblical story and colors its various parts.

It does seem, however, that some of the texts that Barton uses here do not have any narrative influence (Amos 1:3—2:16 and 3:9–21; Proverbs). Especially notable are writings of the prophets and the wisdom literature. But Parry asserts that there is indeed a narrative element present, although indirectly. Amos, for instance, critiques the nations for their injustice. It may be charged that his critique cannot be based on an appeal to the Israelite worldview but must be based on either social convention or on an ethic that transcends particular worldviews.[9] How could he expect these

8. Ibid., 54.
9. Ibid., 54–55.

The Role and Significance of Narrative

peoples to know such moral standards? Parry asserts that, though implicitly, Amos probably is basing his critique on the biblical story of creation.[10] As such, all people are made in God's image and dwell within the same created order. They should possess some idea of certain creational moral norms.

Concerning the wisdom literature, the question is not whether it has a sense of natural law, for it certainly does, but rather if it has any connection to narrative in general and Israel's story in particular. Parry believes it does betray such a connection, though subtly.[11] He finds this in two areas. First, wisdom literature in the Bible is itself based on Israel's story. Proverbs 9:10 states, "The fear of the Lord is the beginning of wisdom." This idea of fear, according to Parry, also includes connotations of commitment to Yahweh within the setting of the covenant relationship. The significance of this is that the wisdom writings of the Bible presume that true wisdom can only be discerned when one fears or understands God rightly, and one can do this only if the work of God in history is understood through Israel's story. Such fear of the Lord is necessary to an adequate understanding of the created order and natural law.

Second, Israel's wisdom literature is deeply interwoven into the other traditions of the covenant people.[12] For example, in Deuteronomy the legal and wisdom traditions flow together: there are laws, framed with the covenantal story, that are written in a wisdom style (Deut 4:6–7). Here also can be found the first hints of a connection between wisdom and torah (Deut 30:11–24 and 32:28–29). Further, there has been some suggestion that wisdom material has helped shape the prophets, especially Amos and Isaiah, and even some narrative material. Genesis 2–3, the Joseph stories, the succession narrative, the Solomon stories, and the book of Esther—these, Parry asserts, all betray a wisdom influence.[13] On

---

10. Ibid., 57.
11. Ibid., 58–60.
12. Ibid., 61.
13. Ibid., 60.

these grounds, Parry concludes that there is good reason to believe that the wisdom tradition is inextricably woven into Israel's story.

Divine Commands

The study of Old Testament ethics has often emphasized law over narrative. To Parry this is a mistake, because it fails to understand the organic nature of the text. In a text such as the Bible, all of the pieces are necessary for the whole. To understand its message one must adequately understand each part and its relation to the others. What this means for ethics is that both narrative and law have their place and must be understood accordingly. Furthermore, the relationship between them is fundamental, for the role and place of one affects the other. Therefore, Parry asks three questions of the relationship between law and narrative: (1) How does the narrative frame of Israel's laws shape them? (2) How does the presence of law within narrative affect the latter? And (3) What is the relationship between law and moral ideals in the Old Testament?[14]

The Narrative Frame of Law

Of primary importance is that Israel's laws are located within the story of the exodus from Egypt and journey to the promised land. Prefacing the Ten Commandments is a reminder of this: "I am the Lord your God who brought you out of the land of Egypt, out of the house of bondage" (Exod 20:2). This reminder reveals that the Ten Commandments, and all the laws that follow, are to be understood with this story in mind.[15] To the biblical reader this truth may seem self-evident, but its significance cannot be understated.[16] Although biblical law at times shows similarities to other ancient

---

14. Ibid., 62.

15. Ibid., 62, quoting Janzen.

16. An important corollary is that, because they are that set within the story of Israel's redemption and covenant with God, the laws become a way by which Israel sustains a relationship with her God. Ibid., 67, following John Walton.

The Role and Significance of Narrative

Near East (ANE) legislation (such as the laws of Hammurabi), it alone is motivated by a historical event.[17] Not only does the narrative frame shape the overall law, but also individual ones. Parry provides examples. Exodus 20:12 reflects the fairly standard ANE idea of honoring one's parents, but gives a unique reason for doing so: "that your days may be long in the land which the Lord your God is giving you." Here is a common ANE ethical idea that is given a new motivation unique to Israel's story. There are also cases where traditional ANE rules are changed to be in line with Israel's story.[18] Slavery, for example, was common in the ancient world. Israel's legislation, however, seems to have more of a humanitarian bent to it (Lev 25:42). The reason for this is located in the exodus, for God calls Israel to treat the slave well because they too had been slaves when he delivered them (Deut 15:15).[19] Clearly, the narrative frame has greatly shaped Israel's law and is necessary to understand it.

The Presence of Law Within Narrative

As the biblical text is an organic entity, not only does narrative affect law, but law affects narrative. Parry sees this happening primarily through the law serving as a guide for morality.[20] It gives the reader parameters by which to evaluate characters as either good or bad, as models for imitation or rejection. Characters become models of either faithful Torah obedience or rebellious disobedience. In this way, the law helps shape the narrative, even as the narrative reinforces the law. Parry offers examples of this organic relationship from the Genesis narratives. There certain characters seem to model Torah obedience (Abel, Noah, Abraham), though

---

17. Parry, *Old Testament*, 63, quoting Sonsino. It should be noted that this statement is limited to cuneiform law; that is, no cuneiform law is motivated by a historical event.
18. Parry, *Old Testament*, 67–68. These adaptations can come in the form of rearranging the priority of moral rules.
19. Ibid., 63–64.
20. Ibid., 64.

the torah had not yet been given.[21] In sum, narrative and law are in a complementary relationship.[22]

Law and Moral Ideals

Last, Parry considers the relationship between law and moral ideals. Here he uses especially the work of Gordon Wenham, who finds that there is indeed a relationship between the two, but perhaps not in the way commonly held. Scholars have often thought that law ought to be the object of Old Testament ethics, because it states the desired ideals. Wenham, however, has suggested that what the law reveals is not so lofty: "law tends to be a pragmatic compromise between the legislators' ideals and what can be enforced in practice."[23] There seems to be a gap between law and ethics: law only reveals what the Old Testament would tolerate, not what it aspired to.[24] But if one cannot find ethical ideals in the law, where would one find them? In narrative, says Wenham, which implicitly reveals Old Testament ideals. To discover these ideals, it is necessary to discern the views of the implied author.

In summary, narrative is essential to Old Testament ethics. Parry seeks to show how this is true by demonstrating the relationship of story to the models of ethics proposed by John Barton: obedience to the declared will of God, natural law, and imitation of God. Wenham introduces the idea that there is a gap between

---

21. Ibid. In *Genesis*, 42–43, Moberly has commented insightfully about this. He suggests that the patriarchs, especially Abraham in Gen 22, are cast in such a way as to show that they were models of Torah obedience in pre-Torah times.

22. Parry, *Old Testament*, 64. Parry also mentions an interesting idea of Calum Carmichael. It is Carmichael's belief that Old Testament laws are often the distilled generalizations of previous narrative traditions. Though Parry does not agree wholesale, he does see value in these views in that they demonstrate the intertwining of law and narrative in ways often unrealized.

23. Wenham, *Story*, 80. See also Wenham's earlier articulation of this in "Gap," 17–29.

24. Parry, *Old Testament*, 65, helpfully points out that the laws Wenham is discussing are only those divine laws that would elicit punishment if broken.

law and narrative, with the former providing the floor of moral behavior, and the latter, its ceiling. These studies show that narrative is not only necessary to ethics but that it also provides a unique contribution.

A UNIQUE CONTRIBUTION

How does narrative contribute in special ways to Old Testament ethics? To answer this question, Parry's work again is insightful. He argues that narrative is distinctively powerful in shaping readers' ethical values. Narrative imprints audiences in ways other genres do not.

Stories offer a unique contribution to Old Testament ethics in their power to form readers. Parry demonstrates that the very nature of human identity lends itself to being shaped by narrative. He establishes theoretical support for his claim from the writings of Paul Ricoeur.[25] Though Parry gives several reasons, only two will be mentioned here. First, the self-identity of each human is storied in form. That is, the idea of the self that each person has is not a collection of principles or abstractions but a collection of stories. Second, and related to the first point, self-identity is not a fixed entity but is always open to molding and formation by experience.[26] These experiences can come in a variety of forms, including stories. The reason stories can supply such experiences is that they provide other "worlds" for the reader to explore.[27] Human identity, in other words, has a natural affinity for stories. This affinity allows for stories to have great influence in the shaping of identity, an influence that other genres do not have.[28]

How does this insight work for ethics? Parry suggests four ways: (1) by exemplifying virtues or general principles of action;

---

25. Parry uses the gamut of Ricouer's work, but he identifies the pillar study on narrative self as *Oneself as Another*.
26. Ibid., 6–7.
27. Ibid., 13.
28. This is not to say that other genres have no influence, but that the matter of their influence is different.

(2) by raising the particularity of specific situations to new heights; (3) by training in emotional perception, which is essential to ethical wisdom; and (4) by refining the very concept of a virtue or duty.[29]

Stories can shape readers ethically by exemplifying virtues and general principles through the lives of characters. Parry discusses the place of model morality in biblical ethics. The Bible has a host of characters that it holds up as examples of behavior. These characters are not meant for wholesale imitation, for often they have vices as well as virtues. What is meant for imitation is a particular behavior of the character in a particular circumstance.[30] Certain actions are considered virtuous in certain situations. Therefore, not every model is meant for every person in every situation. Parry also notes that these characters can at times be generalized for use in other situations.[31]

Stories also develop a reader's particular perception. Particular perception is the aptitude to recognize the unique details of situations.[32] Whereas some ethicists emphasize the use of rules in making ethical decisions, others argue that a capacity to discern elements is more important.[33] In their thinking, real-life situations are too complex and unique to simply apply rules. What it requires is a sensitivity to the individual components of circumstances and the skill to judge how best to respond to them. How might stories contribute to this skill? Parry asserts that stories, like real life, present unique and sophisticated circumstances that require the reader to develop an ability to perceive particulars.

It is not enough to simply perceive particulars; it is also necessary to possess the capacity to construe the situation. At this

---

29. Parry, *Old Testament*, 4.
30. Ibid., 30.
31. For a fuller discussion on this, see Parry, "Greeks," 61–73.
32. Parry, *Old Testament*, 34.
33. See Nussbaum, *Love's Knowledge* and *Poetic Justice*. Nussbaum is the contemporary writer from whom Parry and Barton derive ideas of particularity in ethics.

juncture, Parry introduces the work of Lawrence Blum,[34] who asserts that the ability to properly construe a situation—moral perception—can also be learned through reading stories. Practically, this means that stories help the reader to learn how to discern the nature of circumstances and, consequently, how to make decisions. This has implications for the use of complex characters. Even if such characters are not meant to be imitated, one can learn how to make judgments and decisions by perceiving the particulars of their situations.

Another way in which stories contribute to ethics is by training readers in emotional perception. Emotional perception is the capability to respond with the right sentiment for the situation.[35] For instance, one would expect a person to react in horror at the brutal killing of a child. If, however, a person acts indifferently, one begins to wonder if the person has actually understood the situation. This is because proper moral understanding involves proper emotion. Stories are significant in that they are the primary means for forming emotional response.[36]

How do stories actually shape Christians emotionally? Parry suggests three main ways.[37] First, beliefs (upon which emotion is based) are rooted in the biblical metanarrative. This means that the larger story of the Bible contributes to the values found in each individual story. Second, stories contribute to the larger matrix of emotion. As such, they show appropriate and inappropriate emotional responses. Ultimately, this may influence the reader's ideas of emotional response and create a capacity for such response in the reader. And third, stories may engage the reader so to actually elicit an emotional response. That is, readers get a kind of emotional exercising, whereby they actually feel, for example, anger

---

34. Parry, *Old Testament*, 35.

35. There is some debate as to how emotion and knowledge relate. Parry has a good discussion on the differences between the views of Nussbaum and Roberts in *Old Testament*, 37–41.

36. See Nussbaum, *Knowledge*, 287.

37. Parry, *Old Testament*, 42–43.

or fear. Ultimately, stories help form and deepen one's emotional perception, which in turn contributes to ethical perception.

Parry suggests one more way in which stories contribute to Old Testament ethics: stories can help define virtue and vice.[38] Here Parry uses the term "grammar" to illustrate how this might work: "the grammar of a moral concept is the set of rules, internal to a tradition, connecting and disconnecting it with the other moral concepts within that tradition."[39] He goes on to say that the "grammar of a virtue is a conceptual map of how it links with motives, intentional objects, a concept of human nature, other virtues and vices, and the like." What this means to Parry is that general virtues take on specific form and nuance in the particular stories of each culture.[40] It is, then, within a tradition's narrative structure that each virtue is nuanced and shaped into a "living morality."[41] Another interesting idea should be noted: Stories do not help define virtues by simply exemplifying them; stories also define virtues by relating them to and prioritizing them with other qualities in particular situations.

CONCLUSIONS

It might be helpful at this juncture to summarize the discussed scholars' views on the value of narrative in Old Testament ethics. John Barton holds that the moral importance of biblical stories is not in their commending of virtues or principles. Rather, narrative's value comes from the way in which it portrays human existence and shapes readers' moral imaginations. John Rogerson is also reticent to commend the use of individual tales to extract principles. For him, narrative contributes to Old Testament ethics mainly by grounding and providing examples of the imperatives of redemption and structures of grace. Walter Kaiser believes that

---

38. Ibid., 43.
39. Ibid. See also Roberts, "Kierkegaard," 142–66.
40. See MacIntyre, *After Virtue*.
41. Parry, *Old Testament*, 53.

The Role and Significance of Narrative

narrative can be principlized, though only in light of the legal material. That is, biblical stories are meant to flesh out people's obedience or disobedience to the ideals of the law; principles extracted from the narratives will reflect legal values. Christopher Wright also holds that individual narratives can be principlized (as long as they are understood according to his theological paradigm). Wright argues that by surveying the biblical material, it is possible to construct a portrait of the ideal person. However, he does not articulate exactly how he sees narrative fitting into this survey. Waldemar Janzen, on the other hand, claims that stories are the primary revealer of the biblical idea of ethical living. But he does not think that narrative should be mined for principles or virtues; it should just remain as one unified entity. Robin Parry and Gordon Wenham offer the best proposal. They suggest that individual narratives are the main discloser of Old Testament moral ideals and that from studying those stories one can learn of the virtues commended by the author.

This chapter has examined the issues of narrative's place in and the contribution of individual stories to Old Testament ethics. It argues that narrative is both essential and uniquely contributes to Old Testament ethics. Narrative is essential in that it both forms the foundation and governing structure for biblical ethics and serves as the primary revealer of moral ideals. This latter idea stands in stark contrast to much scholarly opinion, which sees law as the primary revealer of values. Narrative contributes uniquely to ethics mainly in the ways it shapes readers. Four ways have been suggested: (1) by exemplifying virtues or general principles of action; (2) by raising the particularity of specific situations to new heights; (3) by training in emotional perception, which is essential to ethical wisdom; and (4) by refining the very concept of a virtue or duty.

These four points particularly apply to individual narratives, and thus are the primary ways in which they work ethically. Because the aim of this study concerns individual stories and characters, these last four points are especially of interest. Only one, however, is especially helpful for explicit ethical application: the exemplification of virtues or general principles of action. The others are no less true, but they do not lend themselves to concrete application for a number of reasons. Two of them deal only with the shaping of the moral perceptions and processes of one's inner being. The other one, that of stories refining a concept of virtue or duty, only applies in some circumstances. Thus, moving forward this study will focus on discerning the virtues and or general principles of action being commended in particular stories.

3

The Use of Individual Stories

How does one discern the ethical values of individual stories? This chapter follows Gordon Wenham, who proposes three important concepts: virtue ethics, virtue criteria, and rhetorical criticism. Virtue ethics contributes to the task by proposing a certain way of understanding morality, a way that works well with the dynamics of narrative. Virtue criteria establish a system for validating whether or not a behavior is in fact virtuous. They help ensure the reading of the text is in line with the author's intensions. Rhetorical criticism illumines the larger ideology and particular workings of the text itself.

VIRTUE ETHICS

Wenham notes that most discussions about ethical behavior in the Bible have focused on obedience to the declared will of God. Although he grants the importance of this method, he proposes another way for understanding narrative ethically: virtue ethics.[1] Virtue ethics is one of three larger approaches in normative ethics.

---

1. Wenham, *Story*, 88.

The other two are deontology and teleology (consequentialism). In contrast to these, which focus respectively on duties/rules and the consequences of actions, virtue ethics centers on moral character. It emphasizes that the shape of an individual's character enables that person to navigate life's circumstances ethically.

At least three elements are fundamental for virtue ethics: the "good," the virtues, and the community.[2] The good is the supreme end of life. To live virtuously, one must correctly identify the good, for it orders the rest of life. The good establishes for an individual what is worthwhile and deserves allegiance, devotion, and attachment.[3] Conversely, it also determines what is not of value and should not be sought. This ordering of priorities guides behavior. That is, the good shapes conduct by giving life a specific trajectory. It shows what one's "conduct ought to conform to," and is "that from which [one's] living and dying should take its clues."[4] A common articulation of what Christians consider the good comes from the Westminster Confession of Faith: "to glorify God and enjoy him forever."

Virtues are those qualities that allow a person to achieve the good. This is why one's definition of the good is of supreme importance: the identity of the good determines its constituent virtues. For humanity, traditionally four cardinal virtues have been articulated: wisdom, courage, justice, and temperance. Christians have added faith, hope, and love. To possess and exercise these virtues is to live well as human beings. However, there is more to virtue than a list of character traits. Also important are dispositions and intentions. Moral behavior is not limited to what one does; it includes how and why one does it. That is, moral behavior depends on right motivation and manner of acting.[5]

2. Carroll R., "Seeking," 77–96. Carroll lists four elements for his study: the three mentioned above, plus the biblical text, which is a form of tradition used to shape the moral imagination of Christian readers.

3. Birch and Rasmussen, *Bible*, 90.

4. Ibid.

5. For a discussion on the manner of acting, see Hauerwas, *Community*, 113–17. For a discussion on the relation of intentions to virtues, see Hursthouse, *On Virtue*, 121–60.

The Use of Individual Stories

The third foundational element for virtue ethics is the community. The community is important because it is the soil out of which morality grows. Values do not exist in a vacuum; they arise from specific social environs and contexts.[6] Each community holds notions of the good and the virtuous and, in turn, that social group seeks to instill these ideals into its members. One of the ways groups inculcate values in members is through traditions. Traditions may take a variety of forms, but most prevalent and influential is narrative. Through stories, people learn who they are in relation to the larger community and its history; they learn behavior appropriate to the group's ideals.

For the Christian community, the chief narrative is the Bible.[7] It serves as an "identity document,"[8] illustrating uniquely what it means to be the people of God. The enduring sacred story allows contemporary believers to remember their faith heritage and reinterpret it for their own community.[9] This process forms a group character, a shared idea of how values should take specific shape in behavior. One notable way in which the Bible informs behavior is through exemplars. In narrative, exemplars are those literary characters that best embody virtues in their lives. However, it should not be thought that biblical stories intend the wholesale imitation of characters. Rather, it is particular virtues manifested in certain situations that are meant for imitation.[10] This is why figures, such as Abraham, can be both clearly sinful and commended for righteousness. What the narrator commends about Abraham is not the entirety of his behavior, but the demonstration of his faith in his willingness to obey God (Gen 22:18).

In sum, the virtue ethics approach is valuable for the study of narrative because it elucidates the moral dynamics of the text.

---

6. Birch, "Moral Agency," 25.

7. The Bible obviously contains more than just narrative, but the narrative is what coheres the other genres and relates them to the faith community. See Birch, "Moral," 26–27.

8. Carroll, "Seeking," 85.

9. Birch, "Moral," 27.

10. See Janzen, *Old Testament*, 26–45.

Virtue ethics seeks to understand the good of the community that created the stories in order to discern the desired virtues and the trajectory of life. In turn, this information is applied to the details of individual narratives. What emerges is a sophisticated picture of human agency: characters behave in both unrighteous and righteous ways. The unrighteous behavior is meant for avoidance. Readers perceive the wrongful behavior and its negative consequences and are supposed to avoid or purge it from their own lives. Righteous behavior is meant for imitation. Believers ought to emulate the appropriate virtues in their daily behavior.

VIRTUE CRITERIA

In order to properly apply the concepts of virtue ethics to Old Testament narrative, there must be a way of discerning whether or not something is actually a virtue. This is especially true considering that communities tend to define and prioritize virtues differently.[11] Wenham suggests three criteria to verify the presence of virtues: 1) trait repetition; 2) exemplification in a positive context; and 3) alignment with the rest of the Old Testament genres.[12]

It is likely that repeated virtues are meant for imitation. When the narrator wants to communicate a point clearly, he reiterates it. Of course, this does not guard against the replication of negative qualities. To ensure that vices are not mistaken for virtues, Wenham employs his second criterion: usage in a positive context. If a trait appears more than once in a positive context, the reader can be reasonably certain it is meant for imitation. There may be exceptions to this rule, but by and large it will hold true. There is one more way of ensuring a characteristic is truly a virtue: its alignment with the rest of the Old Testament. Because different genres have different emphases, it is important to understand how certain traits are viewed throughout the Old Testament. Such an understanding has two practical effects: the confirmation of virtues and

---

11. MacIntyre, *After Virtue*, 174; See also Birch, "Moral," 25–26; Hauerwas, *Community*, 112.

12. Wenham, *Story*, 88–89.

The Use of Individual Stories

the illumination and nuancing of virtues. The whole council of the Old Testament can come to bear on individual stories.

Wenham uses these criteria to identify virtues and construct a picture of righteous living, an "identikit" of biblical morality.[13] At the base of this moral picture is the virtue of piety,[14] which he defines as prayerfulness, obedience, and dependence on God. However, there is more to the biblical notion of piety than one might think. The pious person, in contrast to common modern opinion, is not weak, but courageous and persistent, both physically and mentally. This courage is not of the violent sort that delights in wrath and fury. Instead, it is one moderated by mercy and justice. To these can be added the virtues of generosity, truthfulness, eloquence, and loyalty. Finally, the righteous person should be characterized by self-control and forgiveness. Interestingly, Wenham notes that things such as emotion and the niceties of life are not to be scorned, but are actually admirable, as long as they are governed by self-control.[15] This, then, is the basic picture of righteous living implied by the Old Testament. Though not exhaustive, it establishes a good foundation for understanding the texts.

The virtue ethics model claims that to properly understand the place and existence of these virtues it is necessary to know their end: the good. It is worth inquiring, then, what the Old Testament might offer as this item. Wenham argues that the legal, psalmic, wisdom, and narrative material hold that peace, good harvests, children, and the presence of God compose the telos of the virtues.[16] However, this illustrates a major problem with defining the good: it is difficult to identify due to its abstract nature. What Wenham in fact articulates are the markers or indicators of the good life, which is the incarnation of the good.[17] That is, he distin-

---

13. This portrait is specifically drawn from Genesis but can be used generally for biblical narrative. See Wenham, *Story*, 100–101.

14. Ibid., 89–91.

15. Ibid., 100.

16. Ibid., 101.

17. Some, such as Barton, argue that the imitation of God is what the Old Testament forwards as the good. However, this is not satisfactory. See Parry,

guishes the features associated with ethical living in the Old Testament. But these are of great value, too. By observing the presence or absence of such markers, it is possible to discern the narrator's commentary on the morality of characters' lives and behavior.

RHETORICAL CRITICISM

The first two of three elements to Wenham's approach are virtue ethics and virtue criteria. The third and final element is rhetorical criticism. Wenham defines rhetorical criticism as an approach that seeks to join the findings of historical and literary criticism to illuminate how a writer in a certain time organized his work to be persuasive.[18] Historical criticism provides the requisite background information, such as the significance of sayings, rites, and institutions; literary criticism analyzes the way in which a piece of writing is put together, including its structure, plotline, and point of view. These two disciplines come together in rhetorical criticism to discern the underlying ideas of the larger work and an author's view of particular behaviors.[19]

The goal of rhetorical criticism is the discernment of an author's opinion.[20] That is, the hope is to be able to understand what the author commends or condemns. In narrative, the way in which these messages often are communicated is through implicit clues from the story's details. To understand the author's opinions one must appreciate his use of story details—how various elements are woven together to create meaning. Wenham's model gives a good point of departure into rhetorical criticism, but his particular ap-

---

Old Testament, 52. Parry rightly asserts that humans can only imitate God to the "extent that [they] image him." Therefore, for people to live rightly, they must behave according to God's specific intentions for the human race. This is why Parry grounds the good in what he calls "creation order" (53).

18. Wenham, *Story*, 3.

19. Ibid., 9.

20. It is important to note that Wenham uses the term "author" as shorthand for "implied author." He follows Sternberg in usually equating the implied author with the narrator in biblical narrative. The goal of narrative interpretation is to discern the stance of the narrator. See *Story*, 10.

The Use of Individual Stories

plication of literary criticism may need some clarification. Though he does not identify details, one may assume from Wenham's work that he employs a kind of case-specific approach. That is, he does not propose a standard or formalized method but adjusts his tools as context demands. This study considers whether it is possible to establish some universally applicable tools.

Robin Parry's work is helpful at this juncture. His idea is to apply an approach that accounts for both a story's formal features and its dramatic movement.[21] In particular, he focuses on two elements: scene division and dramatic peak. By looking at individual scenes and the way in which they are connected dramatically, the reader is able to gain a sense of the story's formal and plot structures.[22] Thus it becomes possible both to discern the significance of individual scenes and to see how they relate to the whole. The other feature, dramatic peak, is important in that it is the story's climax, the event toward which the story builds and then resolves. It provides a watershed moment, linking the first and second halves of the narrative.

These two elements, scene division and dramatic peak, are not meant to stand in isolation. In Parry's system they serve the larger goal of character assessment, which is crucial for reading stories ethically.[23] This is illustrated by his survey of the interpretations of Genesis 34, which shows that the text's moral lessons always are dictated by character assessment. If, for example, Dinah is viewed negatively, as a woman behaving badly, then she is evaluated as an immoral woman, perhaps provoking such an incident. On the other hand, if she is viewed positively, then Dinah is cast as an innocent victim of sexual crime. Thus Parry concludes that proper character assessment is essential for reading narrative ethically.

There are a couple of areas that might be developed further. In addition to identifying a story's individual scenes and climax, one

---

21. See Parry, *Old Testament*, 249–92. Parry's work is largely based on Richard Longacre's discourse analysis ideas, to which he devotes a substantial appendix.

22. Ibid., 124. Scenes are demarcated by change of location, character, or time, by linguistic markers, or by a combination of these.

23. Ibid., 122.

also should seek to understand the plot.[24] Of primary importance is the nature of a story's plot. What is the central tension, and how is it resolved? The way in which these questions are answered determines how the rest of the narrative is understood. Independent of this, though closely related, is another aspect: character choice.[25] The Bible sees people as agents of choice, and so the choices they make are of great importance in revealing their character. Therefore, it is key to ask about the exact nature of a choice, how it came about, and how it relates to the larger plot tension and movement.[26]

CONCLUSIONS

There are three constituent parts to Wenham's approach—virtue ethics, virtue criteria, and rhetorical criticism, all of which work together to bring out the meaning of individual biblical stories. Virtue ethics helps illumine certain moral elements within narrative. It brings to the forefront the concept of virtue. The ways in which different virtues (or vices) impact the lives and behaviors of characters are especially significant. The second constituent part, virtue criteria, helps identify and ensure that certain behaviors are indeed commended as virtuous. This works as a safeguard against reading one's own ideas into the text. The final part, rhetorical criticism, works to discern the ways in which an author crafted the work to achieve the desired message.

Robin Parry's literary method, focusing on characterization, forms a sound foundation for this study. However, it is suggested that modifications are needed. In addition to the elements of scene division and dramatic peak, attention should be directed at plot issues, such as dramatic tension, movement, turning point, and resolution. Character change issues are important also. Combining these various elements brings clarity to the author's evaluation of characters and their behavior, which is crucial for reading narrative

---

24. See the discussion of plot in Gunn and Fewell, *Narrative*, 101–28.
25. Ryken, *Words*, 65–66.
26. See also Ryken, *How to Read*, 52.

ethically. Two additional tools are of great help in understanding characters morally: theme and characterization. The importance of these two tools is discussed at length in the next chapter.

4

Theme and Characterization

This chapter argues that theme and characterization are necessary tools for understanding complex characters, for each meets a particular need. Theme provides a hermeneutic backdrop against which to understand the many details of characters. It also serves as a common thread to unify those elements into a coherent whole. Characterization, on the other hand, functions in a more detailed capacity. It allows the reader to understand the presence and significance of particular details concerning characters. Together, theme and characterization help readers discern the narrator's evaluation of characters.

COMPLEX CHARACTERS

Complex characters present a problem for interpretation.[1] The difficulty arises mostly from their varied nature. Everything from goodness to evil can be seen in one figure in one story. Greatness

---

1. For discussions on character complexity in biblical narrative, see Alter, *Art*, 114–30; Berlin, *Poetics*, 135–39; Gunn and Fewell, *Narrative*, 75–81; and Sternberg, *Poetics*, 321–41.

Theme and Characterization

and failure, charity and greed, honesty and dishonesty—these traits and more may all exist in the same individual. To the literary critic, such portraits are the pinnacle of writing, for they show humanity truly, in all its splendor and horror. However, for the biblical reader, complex characters cause a dilemma, because they obscure the message of the narrator. The question, then, is this: How should characters be interpreted that feature seemingly contradictory signals?

THEME

A main problem with complex characters is that they appear to lack coherence. It is difficult to relate to each other the good, bad, and ambiguous qualities. How should these traits be viewed? Which ones should be considered representative of the actor? What is argued here is that the true underlying issue with character complexity is that it compromises the crucial elements of ethical interpretation articulated in the last chapter: plot issues (dramatic tension, movement, turning point, and resolution) and character change. That is, actors appear to lack coherence because their differing qualities disconnect the characters from the story trajectory.[2] To perceive the significance of confusing details, it is necessary to locate the character in the narrative dynamic. What this means is that a tool is needed to relate the actor's traits to the central plotline. That tool is theme. By discerning a story's theme, the reader is able to better align character qualities with the narrative's purpose.

In common parlance, the term "theme" has a host of connotations. Its use in this discussion is technical. Theme connotes a story's main idea arising from its details, an idea that is usually implied, not stated.[3] It is the rationale behind the content, structure, and development of a literary work.[4] Theme is an abstract

---

2. This is based on the assumption that story details do not exist in isolation; they are meant to be understood in light of the entire storyline.
3. Sage, "Theme," 248.
4. Clines, *Theme*, 18.

Puzzling Portraits

concept growing out of concrete details. Therefore, in contrast to common usage, theme is not the same as subject or motif.[5] Nor is it the same as a story's summary or plotline. Theme is the rationale of these things.

The infamous story of David and Bathseba, in 2 Samuel 11–12, is an example that illustrates this point. Chapter 11 focuses on David's abuse of power: the king commits adultery, tries to cover it up, and ultimately murders Uriah (Bathsheba's rightful husband).[6] Chapter 12 unpacks the destruction wrought by David's sin: Bathsheba's child (produced by the affair) dies, and Nathan prophesies that the king's own household will be ravaged by violence. The subject of the broader story is the consequences of David's abuse of power. A motif that contributes to the subject is the use of the verb "to send" (שלח).[7] Throughout chapter 11, David's abuses of power are highlighted with שלח. Notable occurrences are when David "sends" for Bathsheba (to sleep with her; 11:4), has Uriah "sent" to him (to try to cover up the affair and its subsequent pregnancy; 11:6), and "sends" a letter with Uriah back to the battle (to have Uriah killed; 11:14–15). But chapter 12 develops the "send" motif: God becomes the sender (12:1). Whereas with David "sending" brought about injustice, with God it issues justice. The sending of God's prophet addresses David's sin. The theme, or rationale, behind the subject and motif is: power tends to corrupt character.

Since David is as multifaceted as any biblical figure, 2 Samuel 11–12 provides a good example of the value of theme as it relates to complex characters. Without understanding the story's rationale, it is difficult to grasp how David also could be a man after

---

5. For a good example of "theme" as used to describe concrete features rather than their abstraction, see Amit, *Book of Judges*. Amit holds that signs and leadership are themes in Judges. However, in the strict literary sense, these two items would be considered subjects. For an example of "theme" correctly used in Judges, see Block, *Judges*, 58. Block asserts that the theme of Judges is the "*Canaanization of Israelite society during the period of settlement*" (italics in original).

6. For a discussion of David's abuse of power, see Arnold, *1 & 2 Samuel*, 545–50.

7. For a discussion of the שלח motif, see Alter, *David*, 249–50.

Theme and Characterization

God's own heart (1 Sam 13:14; 16:12) and the exemplar king (2 Kings 14:3). However, in light of the theme ("Power tends to corrupt character"), the reader can relate David's various qualities to the larger plotline. It is revealed that David is not perfect, but neither is he entirely wicked. The text shows that David is man who succumbs to the allure of abusing authority. His son dies, his family will be devastated, and the nation will feel the effects of their king's sin. But David is also a repentant man. At the rebuke of God's prophet, the king humbles himself before the Lord and accepts his punishment. By understanding the story's theme, the reader can understand how to view the narrative details.

Theme is identified in individual stories according to concrete features. David Clines suggests that a reader narrow down the options (based on formal elements) and choose the option that best unifies and explains the arrangement of the various elements. For his own study, Clines does not give an exhaustive list of theme-indicating elements; he simply mentions those applicable to the Pentateuch—namely, motifs and literary endings. Motif is a repeated symbol that represents a thematic idea. Its presence often is a clear indicator of theme. A literary ending also may give a large clue to a story's theme.[8] Primarily, endings point toward the supreme trajectory of the story.

There are three additional elements that are helpful for identifying theme: plot tension, dramatic movement, and literary climax. In the previous chapter, it was discussed how these elements are helpful in discerning a story's rhetoric. They are also valuable in identifying theme. The process of isolating a story's central plot tension, dramatic movement, and literary climax is valuable for finding theme in that it helps explain the relationships between a story's parts.[9] It serves as a bridge between a story's formal elements and its animating idea.

In conclusion, theme aids the interpretation of complex characters in that it connects an individual's traits to the larger storyline. Theme acts as a common thread running through

---

8. Clines, *Theme*, 25.
9. Bar-Efrat, "Some Observations," 190–201.

the narrative; it weaves together the host of seemingly opposing strands. The practical implication is that thematic study enables readers to organize and prioritize character details in relation to the narrative's purpose.

CHARACTERIZATION

There is one more key difficulty with complex characters: understanding how the presence and arrangement of narrative details signal the author's evaluation of characters. The study of characterization helps address this issue. There are two vital areas for the Old Testament. First is the consideration of the general nature of biblical narrative. A broader view of the story's dynamics is needed to give context to particular techniques, because the way in which that narrative sees humans and the manner in which it represents them are fundamental to understanding characterization. Second is an examination of particular techniques. It seeks to answer questions about the concrete ways in which biblical narrative portrays characters. Examples include a story's uses of repetition, speech, and physical description.

The Nature of Biblical Narrative

This section focuses on the work of Meir Sternberg[10] and Robert Alter.[11] These two scholars are pillars in the area of literary approaches.[12] Sternberg and Alter together offer the most comprehensive and thorough discussion on general ideology and specific mechanics of Old Testament narrative. They also hold a traditional understanding of the author-reader relationship. That notion asserts the existence of textual meaning that is discovered by the

---

10. Sternberg, *Poetics*.
11. Alter, *Art*.
12. See Amit, *Reading*; Berlin, *Poetics*; Bar-Efrat, *Narrative*. Technically, Berlin wrote her book (1st ed, 1983) before Sternberg did his, but Sternberg had published a variety of similar works in *Hasifrut* in the 1970s.

Theme and Characterization

reader. It does not, as with some current approaches, place too high an emphasis on the reader's place in creating meaning.[13] For these reasons, Sternberg and Alter provide good discussion partners.

Meir Sternberg

Fundamental to Meir Sternberg's conclusions is one larger idea: the very form of biblical narrative causes readers to experience the same struggle as the characters. The central struggle depicted in the narrative, the struggle for knowledge, is induced in the reader. There is a parallel process occurring between character and reader, with both trying to ascend from ignorance to enlightenment. Sternberg aptly calls that dynamic the "brotherhood of darkness."[14] The very nature of biblical narrative enacts in the reader a drama mirroring the predicament of the characters.[15]

In Sternberg's opinion, the point of this emphasis goes further than just showing humanity's struggle for understanding; it draws a stark contrast between God and the human person, an emphasis unique to Israelite literature.

> Within the Israelite reality-model, briefly, God stands opposed to humankind not so much in terms of mortality—after the fashion of both Orientals and Greeks—as in terms of knowledge. Nowhere in antiquity does the theme of mortality receive so little attention as in biblical narrative; nowhere does the variable of knowledge assume such a cutting edge and such a dominant role.

---

13. See, for example, Gunn and Fewell, *Narrative*, xi. This otherwise fine book leans too heavily on the role of the reader in creating literary meaning. See also Gunn, "New Directions," 412–22.

14. Sternberg, *Poetics*, 48.

15. It should be noted that Sternberg is not without critics. Concerning his ideas on the reader-narrator relationship and on God's omniscience and omnipotence, respectively, see Segal, Review of *Poetics*, 285–86. Segal is much more thorough in her critique of Sternberg, whereas Janzen simply asserts (multiple times) that Sternberg's notions of omniscience/omnipotence are not current with scholarship.

> God is omniscient, man limited, and the boundary impassable.[16]

It may be assumed that in Sternberg's opinion, the primary issue in the Bible is the epistemological, not ontological, difference between God and humanity.[17]

The question that arises is how the story achieves this end. Particulars will be discussed later, but for now it should suffice to mention a fundamental idea: narrative develops in a linear fashion. That is, it progresses sequentially, unfolding moment by moment with each individual event connecting those before and after it. This means that the unique nature of narrative allows for a narrator to manage the way in which details are presented to the reader. The narrator guides the impressions and ideas of the audience; he controls the experience. The way in which a narrator governs the story determines how readers will interpret its events.

There is an important implication of Sternberg's views for narrative ethics. Because of the Bible's emphasis on humanity's inherent ignorance, the focus of characters should be primarily on their decision-making process, and secondarily on the subsequent results. This is because the text, and apparently God himself, assumes humans will do foolish things out of their blindness; mistakes are unavoidable for creatures so limited in knowledge. So the question becomes more about characters' reasons for acting. What were the motivating reasons? On what knowledge did they base their decisions? This is probably close to what Sternberg has in mind when he says that in the Bible knowledge of principles takes priority over knowledge of facts.[18] That is, characters are first evaluated on their principles, and then on the facts possessed.[19]

---

16. Sternberg, *Poetics*, 46.

17. See Damrosch, *Narrative*, especially chapter 2, "History and Epic," 51–87. Damrosch has written an interesting work on the relationship between cultural influences and literary forms. Though not intended as such, his work may lend credence to Sternberg's ideas that the underlying Israelite monotheism gave rise to its unique narrative form.

18. Ibid., 136.

19. See Bar-Efrat, *Narrative*, 61–62.

Theme and Characterization

Such a view would align well with the previously mentioned idea of virtue ethics, in which moral living is not just a set of rules but a process governed by character qualities.

Robert Alter

Perhaps one of Alter's most important points is that Old Testament stories are reticent. In comparison to other literature, biblical narrative features a scarcity of detail about characters.[20] This phenomenon has been described as a sparsely sketched foreground that implies a host of possibilities in the background.[21] That is, the narrator does not articulate the history that gave rise to the character's present circumstances. Rather, he suggests that history through the careful presentation of details. Usually, the Bible reveals an individual's nature by recording gestures, speech, or action. The reader is expected to understand characters based on the subtle clues of bare portraiture.[22]

Like Sternberg, Alter sees this unique narrative not just as a product of style, but as reflective of a larger ideology of the human person.[23] However, his emphases are somewhat different than Sternberg's. To Alter, the central idea is the peculiar relationship between God and humanity, which stems from the larger ideology

---

20. See Berlin, "The Art of Biblical Narrative," in *Poetics*, 135–39; Bar-Efrat, *Narrative*, 48; and Gunn and Fewell, *Narrative*, 63–81.

21. See Auerbach, "Odysseus' Scar," the foundational study on this topic.

22. Also important is the kind of character. Traditional literary scholarship has identified two kinds: flat and round. Recent studies have suggested a third kind: agent. An agent is a character whose function is tied closely to plot or setting, but does not demonstrate personality in itself. A flat character is one that has limited qualities (often only one characteristic). However, a round character displays a host of characteristics. It appears like a real person because of the complex and multilayered composition of its personality. See Berlin, *Poetics*, 32. Berlin rightly asserts that these three character types do not represent different *kinds* of characterization. Rather, they represent different *levels* of characterization; they are points on a continuum of character development. This study is concerned only with round characters.

23. See Gunn and Fewell, *Narrative*, 50, on the importance of understanding human nature for interpreting characters.

of monotheism.[24] Characteristic of this relationship is a freedom that, while assuming a sovereign God, allows for the individual choices and responsibilities of human persons. Alter says it well:

> Every person is created by an all-seeing God but abandoned to his own unfathomable freedom, made in God's likeness as a matter of cosmogonic principle, but almost never as a matter of accomplished ethical fact; and each individual instance of this bundle of paradoxes, encompassing the zenith and nadir of the created world, requires a special cunning in literary attentiveness.[25]

Therefore, the defining characteristic of humanity is its complexity and ambiguity, a fact reflected by the parallel qualities of biblical narrative.

Two more points by Alter are important. On the one hand, there is another significant effect of monotheism on the narrative: each character is seen as part of a divinely guided movement through history.[26] Each is a part of an ongoing chain of God's agents, alike in some ways and different in others, though all connected in the course of God's activity in history. The practical way in which this is shown is through a comparison of characters and their circumstances. Often characters are cast in light of those who have gone before them. A strong clue to actor evaluation comes from the way in which the narrative invites comparison.[27]

On the other hand, there is a significant aspect of the individual narratives: they usually catch characters at pivotal and revealing points in their lives, points that often feature a turning point or change in character.[28] Most individual narratives, then,

---

24. Alter, *Art*, 115.
25. Ibid.
26. Ibid., 60.
27. Cf. Gunn and Fewell, *Narrative*, 48–52, where a warning is issued against seeing biblical characters as simple types. Common, or typal, characteristics must be understood in light of unique ones. Together the two kinds of characteristics create a rounded portrait of the character. See also Bar-Efrat, *Art*, 92.
28. Alter, *Art*, 51.

are meant to have significance beyond themselves; they highlight qualities that typify the lives of the characters.[29] Stories' turning points also take on new significance, for they may show the reasons a certain character's life progressed in a certain way, for good or bad.

Conclusions

Sternberg and Alter offer a number of ideas important to this study. First is the fact that biblical narrative is sparse. It portrays characters with great economy and subtlety. Second, following from the first, the narrative achieves its portraits as much with the omission of information as with its presence. Sternberg calls these omissions gaps. To recognize these gaps is crucial to understanding the narrative. And third, biblical narrative reflects the underlying ideology of monotheism. Sternberg notes the text's emphasis on knowledge over being. The practical effect on individual narratives is that the central struggle deals with knowledge—for characters to move from ignorance to understanding.[30] Alter argues that another result of the underlying ideology is a peculiar freedom for humanity. It manifests in the narrative in the complex and ambiguous choices of humans. The human creature is shown to be both magnificent and wretched.

Elements of Characterization

It has been shown how biblical narrative functions generally. Here the discussion focuses on particular techniques of characterization.

---

29. However, Alter does not believe that characters can be typecast. That is, though the specific narrative might represent the character's larger life, the character is not to be limited to one-word epithets, such as "wily Jacob." Cf. Berlin, *Poetics*, 23–24, 34–37, where Berlin seems to hedge nearer to the notion of typal characters.

30. One does not need to accept Sternberg's ideas wholesale to find value in particular aspects. Here it is accepted that the attainment of knowledge is at least a common theme in biblical narrative.

Puzzling Portraits

The study of characterization is usually divided into two larger categories: direct and indirect. Direct characterization means that an explicit or direct statement is issued by the narrator, such as, "The thing David had done displeased the Lord" (2 Sam 11:27). Indirect, on the other hand, is not straightforward and must be inferred from the presentation of the story details. As compared to direct characterization, indirect confronts the interpreter with a gamut of issues. The goal of this section is to discuss some specific mechanics of indirect characterization in biblical narrative, and to consider their significance.

Reader Positions

Narrative works in a linear fashion, and the way in which the narrator creates meaning is by governing the ordering in which information is revealed. One particular way of managing the narrative is through something Sternberg calls reading positions.[31] What this term describes is the amount of information given to the reader versus that given to the character. Depending on who is given more, different light is cast on the character in the reader's eyes. Sternberg mentions three positions in particular: reader-elevating, character-elevating, and even-handed. The reader-elevating position privileges the reader with more information than the character. Its effect is that the reader tends to see the character in a negative light.[32] An example is 1 Samuel 1:12–16, when Eli mistakes Hannah's lament for drunkenness. The reader is first told of the real situation (v. 13a), which is followed immediately by Eli's misunderstanding (v. 13b). The result is that Eli's poor perception is highlighted in the reader's eyes.

However, the character-elevating position does just the opposite. The narrative advances without the reader knowing why

---

31. Sternberg, *Poetics*, 163–72.

32. Ibid., 164–65. Of course, it can be a fairly complex situation. For example, it may cause the reader to side with one character against another, or side with no characters, or side partially with certain characters and partially with others.

Theme and Characterization

the characters do what they do. Guiding motivations are hidden until the opportune time, when the narrator makes them known to surprise the reader. The purpose of this position is to cause the reader to make a false judgment about the character's motivation. The technique leads the reader to entirely reconsider the actor in light of the new information, which serves to highlight particular character traits. Jonah is a good illustration. It is strange that the prophet flees from God's command (1:3). No reason is made explicit, though the reader may proffer a host of possible reasons. But 4:2 identifies the prophet's real reason: Jonah knows that God's mercy and grace will prevail, and that the people of Nineveh will not be destroyed.

The final position is the even-handed one, in which the character and reader receive information equally. Each struggles at the same pace to make sense of events and circumstances within the story. Usually the use of this device is to bring the reader into the same ignorant state as the character; it highlights the human problem—the disparity between divine and human knowledge.[33] This is exemplified in 1 Kings 3:16–28. Two women who claim motherhood of the same child bring their case to Solomon. Neither the reader nor Solomon is offered more evidence (3:23). It is one woman's word against the other's. What seems to be an irresolvable issue is suddenly and amazingly resolved by Solomon. He commands the child be cut in half, knowing that the true mother would rather have her child alive and with another woman than dead. This example emphasizes God's knowledge over humanity's, in that Solomon has been entrusted with divine wisdom to administer justice (3:12). It is not the man Solomon whose mind accomplishes incomprehensible things; it is the mind of God.

---

33. See Sternberg, *Poetics*, 163, which illustrates how the Bible does this with both negative and positive examples, respectively, with Samuel choosing a king and Solomon judging between the two women claiming one child.

Puzzling Portraits

Literary Gaps

Sternberg is known for his ideas on literary gaps. He believes knowledge is the animating force in biblical narrative; God has it, humanity does not, and the very mechanics of the story show this by creating the same unknowing in the reader. A central way in which it does this is through literary gaps. The notion of gaps is fundamentally simple: story information is purposely omitted to create a desired effect. But the way in which Sternberg sees this working is quite complex. Certain aspects are pertinent to this discussion.

The notion of gaps is dependent on narrative's linear development. According to Sternberg, gaps result from a story's chronological deformity, in which "the order or presentation does not conform to the order of occurrence."[34] That is, the events do not proceed as the audience would expect. This creates in the reader a curiosity about the gaps and a desire to understand or fill them. Subsequently, the reader interprets the story in light of the gaps. It is clear that gaps influence the way narratives are read; but how are gaps helpful for interpreting characters?

For character interpretation, gaps are most valuable when they meet two conditions—when they are relevant to characters and temporary in nature. Not all gaps are helpful for characterization. Some have as their objects items that are only remotely related to story figures. There are, for example, literary lacunae that center on issues of plot, setting, or time. Sternberg mentions the question of what previously transpired between the two prostitutes who were brought before Solomon (1 Kgs 3:16–28).[35] Nothing is said about their prior interactions; the reader is left to wonder. This gap centers on plot, not on character. It may contribute to the overall picture of the story, but it is not immediately helpful for character interpretation. Gaps are most helpful for characterization when their object directly relates to character. They should focus on aspects such as character traits, motives, or

---

34. Ibid., 235.
35. Ibid., 233.

behaviors. Genesis 24:29–31 demonstrates this. Verse 29 records that Laban ran out to meet Abraham's servant, apparently to welcome the man out of hospitality. However, the ensuing verse calls Laban's goodwill into question: it emphasizes that his response was conditioned by the jewelry adorning his sister Rebekah. The gap centers on Laban's motive for acting hospitably. It illumines his character.

According to Sternberg, there are two categories of gaps: permanent and temporary.[36] Permanent gaps are the most difficult to understand, for they are never validated clearly in the text. They are mysterious and perplexing questions left open to the imagination. In 2 Samuel 11, for example, what does Uriah know? Does he perceive that the king is trying to manipulate him? Or is Uriah simply an upright soldier doing his job? Permanent gaps may be legitimate, but they are not immediately useful in the quest to understand characters. Temporary gaps, however, are more helpful. In contrast to permanent gaps, temporary ones do find validation in the text, usually in one of three ways: delayed disclosure, narrative echoing, or opposition in juxtaposition.[37]

Delayed disclosure occurs when the narrator withholds information from the reader, and reveals it later. The book of Jonah is exemplary of this technique. It is the only instance in which a gap controls an entire book.[38] Jonah 1:3 establishes the gap against which the rest of the book is interpreted: why the prophet runs away from God's call. The reader seeks to answer the question throughout the narrative. Sternberg asserts that the impression given to the reader is that Jonah is too tender-hearted to proclaim doom to the city of Nineveh.[39] He would rather run away. In 4:2, however, the reader is jolted by the revelation of Jonah's true motive for fleeing: he knew that God would show mercy and grace to the people of the city. It turns out that wrath is what Jonah did want; he was running from God to try to stop the preservation

36. Ibid., 237.
37. Ibid., 248.
38. Ibid., 318.
39. Ibid.

of Nineveh. Delayed disclosure, then, serves to emphasize Jonah's wrongful ambition.

Narrative echoing functions differently than delayed disclosure. Whereas delayed disclosure is validated by the narrator's eventual filling of the gap, narrative echoing is validated by the characters voicing the very concern implied by the text. That is, the narrative is structured in such a way as to bring a certain question to the reader's mind. To validate the presence of this question, the text puts an identical one into the mouth of a character. An example of this is when Samson demands a bride from the Philistines. His action invites the reader to question whether there is not a suitable bride among the Israelite people. This question is echoed by the text, when Samson's parents ask, "Isn't there an acceptable woman among your relatives or among all our people?" (Judg 14:3). Narrative echoing confirms the presence of the gap about Samson's wife choosing; it highlights a problem with the protagonist's integrity.

The last type of validation, opposition in juxtaposition, is more discrete than the other two. Instead of being explicitly mentioned in the text, it is set up to flag the reader's attention: two contradictory details are recorded side by side. Thus, it is assumed that unless the reader recognizes the discrepancy, there cannot be a cogent account. An illustration of this is in the book of 1 Samuel, in the scene of David's escaping from Saul at night. The narrative records that Michal told David to flee because Saul, her father, was planning to kill him; but when Saul confronts Michal about David's escape, she alleges that David threatened to kill her. Thus a discrepancy is highlighted regarding Michal's two different accounts of the one event. What emerges is a gap about Michal's character. Why did she lie to her father? Was it to keep herself out of the bad graces of Saul?

In conclusion, the importance of literary gaps for characters is that they serve to emphasize and reveal elements important to interpretation, such as traits, motives, and behaviors. Of the two kinds of gaps, permanent and temporary, this study is only interested in temporary ones, because they find validation in the

Theme and Characterization

text. There are three kinds of validation: delayed disclosure, narrative echoing, and opposition in juxtaposition. It is important to recognize that these three types of validation represent a range in certainty. The spectrum progresses from most to least certain: delayed disclosure, narrative echoing, and opposition in juxtaposition. Hence, delayed disclosure offers the best assurance of a literary gap, and opposition in juxtaposition, the least assurance.

Narration and Dialogue

Perhaps the most vital aspect in understanding biblical characters is speech. Alter suggests that the reason for this is that "spoken language is the substratum of everything human and divine that transpires in the Bible."[40] That is, at some level, the Bible sees words as foundational to the directing of events. It is clear that God's words direct things, but so do humanity's, albeit differently. Humanity's use of language is often in less direct ways—to respond to or feel for others, or even to influence or deceive them. Regardless of its use, language is seen in the Bible as the foundation for activity. Thus speech is essential to understanding the thoughts, feelings, and motivations behind characters' actions.

There are many ways in which speech reveals the truth of characters.[41] Three are important to this study. First, the significance of speech is proportionate to its place in the story.[42] For example, the most significant and revealing position for speech is as the first words uttered by a character. The words serve as an exposition of the character, an indicator of what is to come. Second, a lack of character speech can be important. When the narrator says that a character did not respond, or when context emphasizes silence, it should be noted.[43] That silence often exposes a character's inner disposition. The third and final point is that the relation of

---

40. Alter, *Art*, 70.
41. See Bar-Efrat, *Narrative*, 64–77.
42. Alter, *Art*, 79.
43. Ibid.

speech to the rest of the narrative is crucial.[44] This relationship is important in understanding characters because it develops a nuanced and subtle picture of their inner beings.

Central to the speech/narrative relationship is the idea that each element concerns the same event; each renders an account of how the event transpired. In biblical narrative, the narrator is omniscient and inerrant; his words are the standard of truth. When his facts of an event are put alongside a character's, it invites comparison. The ways in which the two accounts either mirror or differ from each other reveals something about the character. A couple of different scenarios are most common. Frequently, there is a subtle divergence between the narrator's report and a character's description of an event.[45] What is revealed about the actor depends on the nature of the discrepancy. Alter uses the example of Jezebel's killing of Naboth in 1 Kings. The narrator records Naboth's death by stoning as the result of trumped-up charges by Jezebel. However, when Jezebel tells Ahab of it, she says, "Naboth is not alive but dead!" The difference serves to show that Jezebel is not concerned with how Naboth is killed. Rather, for her the only important thing is that Naboth is dead. Jezebel's language shows her to be cruel and cunning, unconcerned with anything but her own ends.

An additional scenario is when one character uses another's words. In instances where an actor repeats the words verbatim, it adds weight to the original words and shows the repeating character to be in agreement. More often than not, however, there are slight differences in the repeated language. What this reveals about the character depends on the nature of the wording changes. A good example of this is in 2 Samuel 11.[46] When Joab sends a messenger, he warns the man that David may be angry at the loss of so many men in battle. Joab then gives the courier the message. When the man relays the message to David, however, he changes the wording. The courier softens the death toll and adds other de-

---

44. Ibid., 76–78.
45. Ibid., 77.
46. See Sternberg, *Poetics*, 214–19.

tails about the battle. The manipulation of language shows that the man aims to avoid David's wrath. By reworking the battle report, the courier hopes that the deaths of soldiers will be hidden among the other details. The way in which the words are changed reveals that the courier is just a common man who hopes to avoid the deadly games of kings.

There is one last scenario commonly employed: the relationship between a character's speech and actions.[47] It was no less common in biblical times for people to measure others by comparing their actions and words. The narrative reflects this reality. Much of the material offers no explicit comments on characters' actions alongside speech, because it assumes the implications are obvious.[48] A character whose words and actions align is considered of good integrity.[49] However, if speech and behavior diverge, a lack of moral fiber is inferred. Often at the center of this discrepancy is belief versus action. That is, an individual knows what is proper socially or theologically, but chooses to act otherwise. This draws attention to the fact that the character is ruled by other motivations, such as lust, greed, or rage.

To conclude, Alter's work raises a number of important points concerning the ways in which the dialogue-narration relationship illumines the narrator's commentary on characters. At the base of Alter's view is the centrality of speech. In biblical literature, language is seen as the animating force behind all events; the ways in which humans use words to shape reality betrays their own personal desires and motivations. Formally, the narrative highlights these elements by constructing relationships between narration and speech. There are a few in particular: intentional silence, disparity between speech and narration, disparity between speech and other speech, and disparity between speech and actions. It is suggested that these show the inner realities fueling characters' behavior. They also reveal the narrator's attitude toward those behaviors and their constituent elements.

---

47. See Gunn and Fewell, *Narrative*, 71–75.
48. See Bar-Efrat, *Narrative*, 64.
49. This is true unless a character is consistently bad.

CONCLUSIONS

The tools of theme and characterization address the difficulties of interpreting complex characters. Theme is helpful in that it establishes a center for the wide array of character qualities. It is the common thread that binds together the many strands. Without theme, the diverse details too easily remain islands to themselves; but with it, the reader can relate the qualities to each other and discern their place in the overall trajectory of the story. Characterization, on the other hand, functions to clarify the arrangement and significance of story elements. Because biblical narrative mostly communicates implicitly, it is crucial that the reader understands the rhetorical methods employed. How does the presence of certain elements signal the author's commentary on characters? This is the question that characterization addresses.

The study of characterization has special significance for narrative ethics: it illumines the underlying motivations of characters. A common notion in the work of Sternberg and Alter is that, by understanding character portraiture, a reader enters the inner lives of characters. Those inner realities are important to virtue ethics. They reveal the true reasons for an individual's behavior and provide the audience a nuanced view of human agency. By discerning the motivations and behaviors of which the narrator approves, the reader is able to attain a fuller idea of the kind of person that God commends.

Finally, it should be noted what effects Sternberg and Alter's ideas have on understanding complex characters. This study has assumed complex characters are intended for interpretation. However, it does seem that an additional option exists: at some point complex characters are meant to serve as a message in themselves and not to be untangled. That is, every character may not be meant for complete discernment. Some may be intended to reflect a larger ideology of the human person.[50] That ideology,

---

50. See Bowman, "Complexity," 73-97. Bowman goes so far as to say, "Rather than catalog virtues, condemn vices, and commend a vision of the good life, a biblical character ethics may be limited by the nature of the stories themselves to explain us to ourselves" (75). For a nuanced consideration of

Alter points out, holds that human beings are a tumultuous container of divine and creaturely ambitions.

---

this idea, see Moberly, *Old Testament*, 132–38. Moberly suggests that complex characters can function both as behavioral paradigms and illuminators of the human condition. The options are not mutually exclusive. They can coexist and contribute to the broader picture of morality.

5

Judges 7:15—8:33
An Exegetical Study

It has been argued that to understand characters ethically, rhetoric must be examined. Till now this study has considered specific methods of character examination. Here it will apply those to a specific text, Judges 7:15—8:33, and draw some conclusions. Before this text is analyzed, however, it is necessary to sketch the larger literary units wherein it dwells, namely the book of Judges and the Gideon account (chs 6-8).

JUDGES: AN OVERVIEW

There are two recent studies that have examined the poetics of the entire book of Judges: *The Rhetoric of the Book of Judges* by Robert O'Connell and *The Book of Judges: The Art of Editing* by Yairah Amit. These typically are considered the current pillars of Judges research,[1] and accordingly serve as discussion partners for this

---

1. See, for example, Wenham, "The Rhetorical Function of Judges," in *Story*, 45-71.

study. What will be shown is that though both offer insights into Judges, some elements need to be reconsidered.

Robert O'Connell

For O'Connell, the message of Judges is about kingship, particularly that the right kind of king would help overcome the woes of the judges period. The main questions Judges addresses, then, are: What kind of king? And in what ways would he help overcome the problems? In regard to the first question, the right king would be divinely chosen from the tribe of Judah. What is more, he should not be like Saul nor come from his tribe. In this sense, the book is a polemic against Saul and an apologetic in favor of David. As for the second question, the right king would help solve Israel's problems by exemplifying Deuteronomic ideals. That is, he would expel foreigners from the land and maintain intertribal loyalty to Yahweh's covenant, cult, and social order (i.e., social justice).[2] Therefore, the book of Judges aims to convey that these two characteristics—Judahite descent and covenant obedience—combined in one king would help remedy the woes of the judges period. Its purpose, then, is to convince the readers that Davidic Judahite kingship, and no other, would meet these requirements.

According to O'Connell, the governing ideas of the book can be found in the two- part introduction: 1:1—2:5 and 2:6—3:6.[3] Each part introduces, respectively, one of the two governing schemes: tribal-political or Deuteronomic. The tribal-political scheme establishes an order of tribal/geographic movement for the book: from Judah to Dan tribally and from south to north geographically. Combined with other rhetorical devices, this ordering is meant to show that Judah is preeminent among the tribes. The Deuteronomic scheme establishes the sin-bondage-repentance-restoration pattern so well-known to Judges. Mainly this scheme is concerned with land occupation, intertribal covenant loyalty, cul-

---

2. O'Connell, *Rhetoric*, 10.
3. Ibid., 58–80.

tic order, and social justice. The main purpose of this design is to create a frame by which the events of the time, specifically judges' actions, could be evaluated morally and religiously.[4] Together these two schemes provide the governing ideas and structure for the whole of Judges.

Methodologically, O'Connell focuses on both structural and thematic features in Judges. For structural qualities, he emphasizes formal arrangements and motif patterning, and for thematic ones, plot structure and characterization. Most important of the formal arrangements and motifs are the tribal-political and Deuteronomic schemes already mentioned. There is, though, one more aspect that should be discussed: the hermeneutic priority of these two schemes. Though it is true that the structural and thematic features work together to form the message of Judges, the larger structural ones (i.e., the two schemes) take interpretive priority. The reason for this is simple: these structures create the framework within which the thematic features find their meaning. In a way, they define the boundaries inside of which the thematic features dwell and the moorings to which they are anchored.

Of the many ways to study thematic features, O'Connell chooses two that are especially fitting for Judges: characterization and plot-structure.[5] Characterization itself has many facets, but his focus is on the device of narrative analogy. Narrative analogy is a kind of intentional parallelism that invites comparison between two items. In the case of Judges, it occurs at various levels, namely between a deliverer and the larger population, and between a deliverer and Saul. Analogy between a deliverer and the populace typically serves to show that there are corresponding deficiencies in Israel and her deliverers. In this sense, a deliverer exemplifies the larger problems of the nation. Analogy between a deliverer and Saul, however, tends to show that the covenant compromises of the deliverers will also be characteristic of Saul. This, then, means that the analogies of the deliverer accounts aim, first, to exemplify the chronic disobedience of the times and, second, to show that

---

4. Ibid., 20.
5. Ibid., 80–81.

Saul's leadership would be plagued by many of the same issues as the judges.

Concerning plot-structure, O'Connell observes that most exegetes study stories according to their scenic elements (scene division, etc.). The problem is that in doing so they may be running roughshod over important contours of the storyline. Therefore, he proposes an approach that analyzes the development of the different "plot levels." Plot level, according to O'Connell, concerns the literary growth of a theme rooted in the circumstances of the narrative.[6] Every story has a theme, which is usually revealed in the introduction. Themes, however, are not static but undergo change and maturation as a tale progresses. In fact, it is fairly common for a narrative's development to spawn new themes, known as subplots, which are also important to the resolution and message of the story. Therefore, O'Connell's approach seeks to identify the plot level (or levels) of the narrative and to discern how its growth and resolution contribute to a story's larger message. A major part of this is examining the way in which a story is organized to achieve one main purpose. Once this is done, it is possible to identify the implicit ideals by which the characters and events are measured.[7]

To conclude, O'Connell suggests that the message of Judges is that the right kind of king would remedy the woes of the judges period. The proper king would be God's chosen, from the tribe of Judah, who would uphold the Deuteronomic ideals of driving out foreigners and maintaining intertribal loyalty to Yahweh's covenant, cult, and social justice. Rhetorically, the book accomplishes this through using several devices. First, the introduction establishes the main ideas and structure of the book through two schemes: tribal-political and Deuteronomistic. These set the stage for the literary and theological development of the book, and they establish the hermeneutic frame by which to interpret the individual deliverer accounts. They show generally that Judah is preeminent among the tribes and that the judges period would be one of awful decline. Second, the individual narratives employ analogy,

6. Ibid., 5.
7. Ibid., 4–5.

between both deliverer and populace, and deliverer and Saul. As such, it becomes clear that most of these deliverers are negative examples of Yahwistic piety, and their failings are both characteristic of the larger populace and of the later reign of Saul. Third and last, the conclusion fleshes out the message of the whole book. Whereas stories of specific individuals characterize the body of Judges, the conclusion is void of such characters, with anonymous characters filling the scenes instead. The purpose of this shift is to show that individual behavior has nationwide effects and parallels. That is, the godless behavior typical of the deliverers has now become typical of the nation, penetrating into the very fabric of religious and social life. As such, the themes of cultic apostasy and social disintegration, central to the deliverer accounts, are fully developed and displayed in the conclusion. At the close of Judges, Israel is adrift without direction.

Yairah Amit

According to Yairah Amit, the message of Judges is that a new kind of leadership is needed to resolve the problems of the period, and kingship is that leadership. It is not so much that kingship itself is seen as ideal, for it is not, but that it meets criteria necessary to Israel's success. That is, the nature of monarchy as an institution lends itself to resolving the issues of that period, at least better than does the rule of judges. Two aspects are needed for successful rule: an "internal mechanism for continuity" and sound criteria for choosing leaders.[8] Neither aspect is met in the rule of the judges, though in monarchial rule they are realized at least in part. The reason these aspects are important is because, according to Amit, Judges shows their absence as large factors in the disobedience and rebellion of Israel in the judges period. The purpose of Judges, then, is to convince readers that monarchial rule is the best option available for getting Israel back on track covenantally.

---

8. Amit, *Book of Judges*, 92.

For Amit, two ideas undergird the whole of Judges: signs and leadership. Both are fundamental to the structural and thematic development of the book, and both aim to answer the book's central questions. The sign theme was meant to answer questions about God's involvement with Israel during this period. Its presence shows, first, that God was indeed active in guiding Israel, and second, exactly how he was active. It accomplishes this goal by employing two kinds of signs: direct and indirect. Direct signs are what can be considered divine manifestations, such as the appearance of angels and occurrence of miracles. Indirect signs, however, come not from individual events in time, but from an overall view of these events, which reveal the activity of God. In Judges, this means that the cyclical nature of the period was not just the normal ebb and flow of history, but the dynamic interaction between Israel's failing and God's saving.

The leadership theme was meant to address questions about the governance of Israel, specifically concerning how the monarchy came about.[9] Its answer is that the monarchy came about because of the need for a new kind of governance. The way in which it depicts this need is by characterizing the judges period as one of steady and steep decline. As the book progresses, the leaders become increasingly worse. By the end, the reader is left thinking that something must be done to save Israel from national destruction. As already shown, though, the answer is not simply to find better leaders but to find a better governing system. Thus, the monarchy.

Amit's ideas of composition are largely based on the linear development of narrative.[10] That is, she pays great attention to the sequential ordering of narrative, because it determines the way in which readers experience and, therefore, interpret texts. Practi-

---

9. In Amit's scheme, the leadership theme is primary and the signs theme secondary, which ultimately means its subservience. As such, even the signs theme is used to answer questions regarding leadership. Most notably, it works to negate the idea that the monarchy was sought because of a lack of God's presence.

10. In this sense, her ideas follow closely to Sternberg's, which were discussed earlier.

cally, this means Amit is especially interested in the impact that ordering has upon a story's thematic development.

Amit sees the ordering of Judges contributing to and developing the major theme of kingship.[11] In general, she sees two larger parts to the body of Judges (3:7—8:35 and 10:1—16:31). The first part is made up of one group, the delivering judges,[12] and the second part of two groups, the consecutive[13] and disappointing[14] judges. Characteristic of the delivering judges is that each is known by a single act of deliverance; afterward very little is told about his/her life and leadership. Most importantly, it seems the writer of Judges meant to show that the very presence of these deliverers ensured peace for Israel (2:16, 19). True to their name, the consecutive judges' characteristic is that they were consecutive leaders, part of a larger chain. Of notable importance in these narratives is that two items parallel each other: consecutive leadership and lack of apostasy. This, according to Amit, invites the reader to assume that the reason for peaceful times without apostasy is a result of consecutive leadership. And last, the disappointing judges share the characteristic of failure to act rightly. What makes these judges so disappointing is that each has great potential but falls into horrible sin. Their location also emphasizes failure, for each appears after one of two consecutive leader sequences. That is, the failure of Jephthah and Samson looks quite stark when juxtaposed with the success of the consecutive judges.

Each group of judges serves a unique role in the book's composition. The reader first comes across the delivering judges (Othniel, Ehud, and Deborah in 3:7—5:31), who offer a fairly good example of leadership and whose very presence ensures times of peace. Acting as a transition between the delivering and consecutive judges are the Gideon and Abimelech stories (6:1—9:57), both of which deal with the issue of kingship.

11. Amit, *Book of Judges*, 76–92.
12. Othniel through Gideon.
13. Tola, Jair, Ibzan, Elon, and Abdon.
14. Jephthah and Samson.

Judges 7:15—8:33

Gideon's story offers the ideal—that Yahweh should be king—and Abimelech's reveals the horrors of bad kingship. Together they bring the reader to consider kingship in balanced, honest terms. Immediately afterward, the consecutive judges are introduced (Tola and Jair in 10:1-5, and Ibzan, Elon, and Abdon in 12:8-15) punctuated by the disappointing leadership of Jephthah (10:6-12:7) and Samson (13:1-16:31). The consecutives emphasize the value of constant leadership. The disappointing judges, however, are meant to show that, though the deliverers at the beginning of the book did fairly well leading, they did not do enough; a better kind of leader is needed. Therefore, what Amit sees the composition of Judges doing is gradually unfolding both the question and its answer. That is, when the reader realizes no judge will do and asks what kind of leader would work, the idea of kingship has already been incubating. The reader sees that, though kingship is not perfect, it is the best solution to the meet the criteria of choosing leaders and having constant leadership.

Amit's method is perhaps not as clear as O'Connell's, but is discernible nonetheless. Her goals are to uncover the compositional principles that guided the editors of Judges and to discern both the choice and organization of the material.[15] It is, then, not very different from O'Connell's method. Amit first focuses on the underlying ideology and then analyzes the formal structures and patterns. Together these items form the larger interpretive structure, by which the smaller pieces are understood and the larger message discovered. Where O'Connell and Amit do differ is in their conclusions concerning the significance of the larger structures and patterns, and also in their approach to the individual narratives.

In summary, for Amit, Judges portrays Israel's problem, which is apostasy due to lack of leadership, and also gives the answer to that problem, which is kingship. Kingship, however, is not held up as ideal. Instead, it is seen as a practical solution to a chronic problem. In fact, kingship in itself holds no intrinsic value other than the fact that it is a governing system that meets certain

---

15. Amit, *Book of Judges*, xvi.

criteria. These criteria are better standards for choosing leaders and constant/consecutive leadership. The way in which Judges accomplishes its message is by portraying the growing problem and, all the while, gradually introducing kingship as the answer. Judges also argues against other competing ideas, such as that Israel's problems are due to Yahweh's absence. It does this by showing that he was active in the judges period, and that in spite of this Israel still managed to go astray. Thus Judges carefully moves to demonstrate the true reason for Israel's problems and to offer a solution.

Critical Interaction

Most important to this discussion are two emphases of O'Connell and Amit: Judges' underlying ideals and its organization to achieve the intended message. These emphases are uniquely important to Judges, because its very existence is built upon individual stories. These would have required organizing and structuring to form a coherent whole.[16]

O'Connell suggests the organizing principles are the tribal framework and Deuteronomic cycle, and Amit the themes of signs and leadership. Though on the surface these may seem different, their end is similar: the commending of kingship. Of course, each tends to emphasize different aspects of kingship—O'Connell the kind of king and Amit the kind of institution. But overall, it seems they would mostly agree. However, each understands the book's organization differently. In O'Connell's opinion, the introduction reveals the themes in raw form, the body fleshes these out with specific examples, and the conclusion rounds out and ties the ideas together. Everything necessary to the book can be found in the introduction, albeit in seed form, and there are no fundamental surprises. This is not the case with Amit's scheme. From her perspective, the introduction does reveal the major issues of the book,

---

16. Nearly all scholars would agree on this point. See, for example, Younger, *Judges*, 23, and Soggin, *Judges*, 5–6. Each represents a different theological tradition, though each would agree that Judges is composed of various parts. What would be different are their views on the nature and use of those sources.

but not their answer. The answer is gradually unveiled as the book progresses. Through a complex and subtle arrangement of details, the book warms the reader to the idea of kingship.[17]

However, O'Connell and Amit's views about the rhetoric of Judges need adjustment to be satisfactory. Three scholars offer ideas helpful for this modification: Lillian Klein, Barry Webb, and Daniel Block. Klein suggests that what undergirds Judges is a difference in perspective between Yahweh and Israel.[18] In her view, the narrative is arranged in such a way as to highlight that each party has different desires.

Yahweh desires primarily that Israel be obedient to him and the covenant, but Israel desires above all the fruit of that obedience, which is possession of the land. As the book unfolds, this disparity and its consequences are explored. What is clear is that a parallel exists between Israel's wrong desire and their poor behavior. To the extent that Israel has misplaced desires, she will also have misplaced priorities. The typical result is a shift in values: Israel begins to value power and possessions above ethics and people.[19] Awful are the consequences, and they stand in stark contrast to Yahweh's desire.

Other than highlighting the disparity in perspectives, Klein asserts Judges' structure has another function: to demonstrate Israel's national identity. It is no accident that the number of judges is twelve, for together the judges represent all of Israel.[20] Each judge is an individual and has unique weaknesses, but ultimately each represents the larger failings of the nation. As Judges continues, there is a fuller picture of the problems in Israel, all of which

---

17. Amit's scheme basically depends on two features of narrative arrangement: the order of presentation and overall location of crucial details. Though the issue of kingship does not surface early or often in Judges, it is strategically linked to central motifs—strife and apostasy—and employed at crucial junctures. The significance is that, though not mentioned often, the idea functions as if it were central all along, and the natural answer to the problem at hand. For the specific workings of this dynamic, see Amit, *Book of Judges*, 76-119.

18. Klein, *Triumph*. For a synopsis of her views, see 12-21.

19. Ibid., 18. On this view, Klein cites Mendenhall, *Tenth Generation*, 225.

20. Klein, *Triumph*, 16.

contribute to a growing chasm between the nation and their God. It should be noted that in contrast to O'Connell and Amit, Klein does not see an argument for kingship in Judges. She agrees that the book laments the lack of good leadership and emphasizes the need for a righteous leader.[21] However, such a situation does not demand a king. In fact, she argues that the only mention of kingship comes from Israel's perspective, which is directly opposed to Yahweh's. Therefore, the book does not reflect a desire for a king, who would be of Israel's choosing, but instead points to an obedient and righteous leader, who would be of Yahweh's choosing.

Webb argues that the main issue in Judges is Israel's failure to take the whole promised land.[22] Its composition aims to answer the question of why Israel has not come to possess the land, as Yahweh promised the patriarchs. The answer is given in the introduction and further developed throughout the book: Israel's apostasy is what caused the failure to possess the land. Yahweh has kept his end of the covenant, but Israel has not kept hers. Similar to O'Connell and Klein, Webb sees Judges' introduction laying out the main dramatic tensions and the body developing them. Also, he believes the book records the progressive moral degradation of Israel, which is demonstrated by a parallel movement in the judges.

Another important element of Webb's work is his understanding of Judges' place within the so-called Deuteronomic history.[23] Far from evincing a "simplistic moralism or a mechanical theory of history," Judges displays a complex dynamic between the chosen-though-failing Israel and her merciful-though-just

---

21. Ibid., 141.

22. Webb, *Book of Judges*, 121–22.

23. The term "Deuteronomistic History" refers to the canonical books of Deuteronomy through 2 Kings, which generally are understood to record Israel's history in light of her obedience to the stipulations of the Sinai Covenant. Israel's course, in this vein of thinking, predictably proceeds according to whether or not she is obedient to the covenant. The classic study was done by Martin Noth in 1943: *Überlieferungsgeschichtliche Studien*. The English translation was published in 1981: *Deuteronomistic History*. For a recent summary of this term, see Richter, "Deuteronomistic History."

God.[24] What results is a portrayal of Yahweh as entirely free and at times unpredictable. Though Yahweh is merciful, Israel cannot be sure that calling upon his name will always guarantee deliverance. Sometimes Israel must wallow in her sin. Such an idea removes the simplistic notions about Judges and places it in the company of books like Job, in which Yahweh is far less predictable than thought.[25]

Block contends that Judges needs to be understood differently than it often is.[26] First, there needs to be a reconsideration of Judges' genre. Instead of the book being understood as a political tractate, it should be seen as a prophetic work. He points out that Judges' canonical location places it squarely in the former prophets. Second, there needs to be a better understanding of the actual role and function of the judges. Though most have attributed religious responsibilities to the judges, Block argues that, due to scant evidence, this is mistaken. What is more likely is that the judges were meant to address the *effect* of Israel's sin, not its *cause*. That is, they were supposed to fight off the foreign oppressors that had been brought by the nation's sin, not to religiously reform the nation.

The aim of Judges, in Block's opinion, is to sound a prophetic call for the people to return to Yahweh. It communicates this message by showing the "Canaanization of Israelite society" as a result of the nation's disobedience.[27] Israel is in a freefall as a direct result of her sin. It is not clear what kind of repentance and return Block believes Judges is looking for; perhaps it was to be a national repentance. What is clear, though, is that he does not see Judges forwarding kingship as the answer to Israel's problems.[28] In reality, Block holds that the ideology serving as Judges' founda-

---

24. Webb, *Book of Judges*, 209–10.
25. For the full discussion of this idea, see Polzin, *Moses*.
26. See his commentary, *Judges*, and especially his article, "Period of the Judges," in *Israel's Apostasy*.
27. See Block, *Judges*, 58. This is in fact what Block believes Judges' theme to be.
28. Contra O'Connell and Amit.

tion is Gideon's rejection of human kingship. Therefore, in Block's opinion the book of Judges is intended to call Israel back unto her God by way of showing her the consequences of sin.

Conclusions

O'Connell and Amit offer valuable insights on Judges, but their views need to be honed with those of other scholars. From O'Connell, perhaps the most valuable idea concerns the unfolding of the book. He rightly suggests the introduction (1:1—3:6) lays out the fundamental themes and dramatic trends of the book, the body (3:7—16:31) develops and nuances them, and the conclusion (17:1—21:25) ties them up and shows their ultimate effects. However, the themes O'Connell puts forward need to be reconsidered. It is true that the ideas of cultic and tribal fidelity are central to Judges, but it may be better to subsume them under Block's larger theme: the Canaanization of Israelite society.[29] Further, it would be good to understand that these themes are not necessarily tied to kingship ideology.

Amit's assertion about the progressive revelation of Judges' ideology (concerning kingship) is sophisticated and well-thought-out, but unlikely. What is more likely is that there does exist a progression of revelation within the limits already set by the introduction. Klein and Webb are helpful here. Both mention a parallel trend of moral worsening as the book progresses. Though Klein's notion about differing perspectives may be a little forced, her thoughts on Israel's shifting values are right on the mark. As the nation loses touch with Yahweh's call, it begins to value material and carnal things above righteousness. Poignant is Webb's point that it is not only the nation but also the judges that grow worse morally. In fact, Webb has shown a parallel movement downward between judge and nation; as the judge goes, so goes the nation. Lawson Younger has also contributed to this idea. He contends

---

29. It should be noted this idea fits very well with Webb's notions of Judges' larger workings.

that Judges features an inclusio structure that emphasizes a certain pattern of degradation:[30]

> Foreign wars (1:1–2–5)
> Foreign idols (2:6–3:6)
> Domestic idols (17:1–18:31)
> Domestic wars (19:1–21:25)

The significance of this pattern is that it illumines the process of degradation. With issues of idolatry in the middle, it may be assumed that idolatry represents the point at which corruption moves from outside of Israel to within it. Coupled with Webb's idea of the parallel movement between judge and nation, it predicts that the tide turns for the worse for Israel when its judges begin to commit idolatry.

Klein's idea about the twelve judges representing the whole of Israel is important. In her scheme, the judges assume both individual and corporate significance. Each judge functions as a microcosm of the larger nation. At one level, the judge is part of the whole, and his failings contribute to the failings of all Israel. On another level, each judge is also representative of the nation, and his particular vices symbolize those characteristic of the rest of Israel. What this means for the so-called minor judges is that they function mostly to round out the judges' number to twelve. They are not in themselves meant to hold significant literary value. This is contra Amit, who gives minor judges a rather large place in the book's rhetoric.[31]

In summary, it seems best to see Judges as a symphony.[32] Its overture (1:1—3:6) introduces the major themes, its variations (3:7—16:31) develop and nuance them, and its coda (17:1—21:25)

---

30. Younger, *Judges*, 31.

31. It is spurious whether, as Amit claims, characters with insignificant literary roles can hold significant thematic roles. It seems she places too much emphasis on the motif of consecutive leadership (as she defines it), and finds it in places where it really is not.

32. This is the analogy used in Webb, *Book of Judges*, and the structure by which Webb orders his book.

brings them to final fruition and closure. The themes introduced by the overture revolve around Israel's failure to fully attain the promised land. Especially evident is that Israel is becoming more and more Canaanized due to her apostasy and idolatry. This results in a corruption of values: from valuing justice and people to valuing power and possessions. The variations section further reveals that it is not just the lay people who are going astray, but also Israel's judges. As the judges themselves indulge in sin, the corruption spirals out of control on the national level. In the coda, the fullness of Israel's sin is manifest. Tribe wars against tribe, and the office of priest is defiled horribly. It was noted that such a view of Judges does not necessitate the presence of a dominant kingship ideology. Though kingship ideology may be present, it is subservient to the larger message of repentance and return to the Lord through covenantal obedience.

JUDGES 6–8: THE GIDEON STORY

Scholars are divided over the role and function of Gideon's account in Judges. Some, such as Amit, see Gideon positively and assert he is an exemplary judge.[33] Most others, however, see him much differently. Though the exact function of Gideon's account is debated, it is agreed that he should be viewed negatively. Webb attributes to Gideon some credit for his initial behavior, though ultimately it is overshadowed by his poor actions later in life.[34] O'Connell holds that Gideon is a flawed hero, whose failings become writ large in his son Abimelech. Block believes the narrator aims to show Gideon as a man of hypocrisy.[35] Klein argues Gideon is meant to strongly contrast the piety of Moses, the servant of God.[36] Elie Assis proffers that Gideon is ruled by selfish ambition

---

33. Amit, *Book of Judges*, 235.
34. Webb, *Book of Judges*, 151–52.
35. Block, "Will the Real," 353–66.
36. Klein, *Triumph*, 51.

and lacks genuine faith in Yahweh.[37] It is clear that the majority of scholarship views Gideon in a negative light. What role, then, does his account play in Judges?

In 1982, D. W. Gooding wrote an important article on the structure of Judges.[38] In it he argued that the composition of Judges betrays a chiastic structure, for which he offered a detailed outline. It now seems his structure was somewhat overstated, but what remains is his idea about the place of the Gideon account. This account, he argued, is the turning point of the whole book.[39] From Gideon on, there is a marked decline in the judges' moral character. It is no longer just the people who engage in sinful behavior, but also the judges themselves. Thus the Gideon account serves as a pivot for the whole of Judges.

Many scholars have accepted this idea and used it in their own work.[40] However, there is still disagreement concerning the nature of the Gideon account itself. Two areas are especially important: structure and theme. Concerning structure, Amit has shown the account can be divided into two larger blocks: 6:1—7:23 and 7:24—8:33.[41] Each block represents a distinct phase in the story, which differs from the other in both theme and rhetoric. Amit asserts that the first block reflects the theme of signs, and the second block that of leadership. Rhetorically, the two blocks differ mainly in the areas of geography, time, and characterization.[42] As far as geography is concerned, the first block centers around events on the west bank of the Jordan, and the second on events on the eastern side. The two blocks differ in their usage of time in that the former heavily emphasizes the sequence of events, whereas the latter gives

---

37. Assis, *Self-Interest*, 120-21.
38. Gooding, "Composition," 70-79.
39. Ibid., 74.
40. See, for example, Exum, "Centre," 412; Tanner, "Gideon," 150; Klein, *Triumph*, 50-51; and Assis, *Self-Interest*, 100.
41. Amit, *Book of Judges*, 232. Amit's actual structure only goes through 8:27a. However, vv. 27b-33 are included here for the sake of clarity and to avoid a lengthy discussion on Amit's editorial views concerning Judges.
42. Ibid., 238-44.

little attention to chronology. And in regard to characterization, the first block portrays Gideon as constantly fearful, and God as constantly active in bringing out his purposes. The second block, however, shows Gideon as resolute and certain, and God as absent except in Gideon's words.

It is agreed that two of Amit's points are partially true. On the one hand, there do seem to be two distinct blocks in the Gideon account (though each may benefit from modification). On the other hand, it is also true that the blocks reflect the unique rhetorical characteristics discussed by Amit. What is not certain, however, is the presence of her two themes: signs and leadership. The reading offered here suggests that these fail to adequately account for the dramatic movement of the Gideon account and the integration of its various elements.

Previously it was argued that three pieces are necessary to discern a story's theme: scene division, plotline, and turning point. The way in which these pieces interrelate determines theme. Amit holds that block one has eight scenes (6:1-10; 6:11-24; 6:25-32; 6:33-35; 6:36-40; 7:1-8; 7:9-15a; 7:15-23) and block two, four scenes (7:24-8:3; 8:4-21; 8:22-27; 8:28).[43] These are generally acceptable.[44] She asserts that the plotline revolves around the conflict with Midian and, accordingly, that conflict's turning point (7:23) serves as the overall story's turning point. These, however, need to be reconsidered.

Regarding plotline, it appears that the governing dramatic tension is Gideon's struggle to believe Yahweh, not his conflict with Midian.[45] Evidence for this can be found in at least three areas. First, motifs in the account relate more directly to the issue of

---

43. Ibid., 224-25.

44. Differences do exist with the view of this paper, though not ones significant enough to warrant mention. For reference sake, the scene divisions accepted here are as follows: 6:1-6; 6:7-24; 6:25-32; 6:33-35; 6:36-40; 7:1-8; 7:9-14; 7:15-25; 8:1-3; 8:4-9; 8:10-14; 8:15-21; 8:22-27; 8:28-35. They are based on the typical factors of scene demarcation: formal markers and change in character(s), subject, or setting.

45. A good discussion of this is in Tanner, "Gideon," 156-57.

Gideon's relationship with Yahweh.⁴⁶ Second, the book of Judges is not about foreign conflict, but Israel's disobedience. Oppression comes as a result of disobedience; it is therefore secondary to the relationship between Yahweh and his people. Foreign conflict simply sets the stage for the true drama between Israel and Yahweh.⁴⁷ And third, the issue of the Midianite conflict is resolved early in the narrative,⁴⁸ whereas that of Gideon's disobedience continues throughout, and is even the necessary link to the Abimelech account. It would be surprising if the account treated its main plot tension in such a way. Therefore, it seems the plotline revolves around the issue of Gideon's struggle to trust Yahweh and his subsequent disobedience.⁴⁹ Accordingly, the dramatic turning point also needs to be refigured. Tanner rightly notes that the tipping point for the story is 7:15: "When Gideon heard the dream and its interpretation, he worshiped."⁵⁰ Here Gideon's fear is resolved, and never again does he struggle with doubt. What Tanner fails to note, however, is the significance of the marked change in Gideon in the second block.⁵¹ In place of fear, the second block features the motif of resolute violence and brutality and an emphasis on Gideon's idolatry and foreign liaisons.⁵² The subject, it is argued, is Gideon's immoral living.

---

46. Ibid., 158.

47. As such, the Midianite conflict may be seen more as a part of setting than plot.

48. Technically, it ends in 8:21. Effectually, however, it ends in 7:21 with the phrase, "all the Midianites ran, crying out as they fled." From here forward, the narrator only records details of the conflict summarily, which gives the impression that the battle is over.

49. There are also other elements supporting this idea, such as the fact that the individual scenes—their subjects, themes, and integrating factors—seem to point in the same direction.

50. Tanner, "Gideon," 158.

51. The new blocks would be 6:1–7:15a and 7:15b–8:33. See Assis, *Self-Interest*, 16–17. Assis does not actually divide v. 15, but ends with it and begins the next block with v. 16. The intent and result are the same, however.

52. Gooding, "Composition," 74–75, mentions tribal brutality and idolatry, but not foreign liaisons.

The connection between the elements of turning point, plotline, and block subjects points toward a different theme than those proposed by Amit.[53] In the first block, the subject is Gideon's struggle to believe Yahweh, and in the second, his immoral living. They are linked by the turning point (7:15a), where Gideon is said to believe and worship. The tension is obvious: though Gideon is said to worship, he proceeds to live a horribly immoral life, one that is neither pleasing to nor reflective of Yahweh's wishes. This implies that the transformation is somehow incomplete. Gideon does overcome doubt, but fails to worship Yahweh in the truest sense. To strengthen this notion, it should be noted that the turning point only says Gideon worshiped, but not who or what he worshiped. There is a purposeful ambiguity here. Thus the resulting theme of the Gideon account is this: the consequences of impure belief.

In conclusion, it has been argued that Gideon should be interpreted negatively. His account functions as the dramatic axis of Judges. For the first time in the book, a judge takes part in the degradation. No longer is it just the people who sin, but also the leadership. The trend begins with Gideon and grows worse as the book progresses. Three sins particularly characterize Gideon: idolatry, intertribal brutality, and foreign liaisons. Contrary to popular opinion, the account does not revolve around the Midianite conflict. Instead, its dramatic movement reflects Gideon's struggle to believe Yahweh. Once he does believe, however, a new set of problems is introduced, ones dealing with immoral character. This dynamic implies an ambiguity in his act of worship, which gives rise to the overall theme: the consequences of impure belief. The Gideon account aims to show the havoc brought about through Gideon's lack of belief.

---

53. Strictly speaking, Amit's themes seem more like block subjects.

JUDGES 7:15—8:33

Judges 7:15—8:33

This block comprises the second half of the Gideon account. In 7:15, Gideon worships and overcomes his issue of doubt. However, a new issue is introduced. In 7:16–8:33, new questions arise about the nature of Gideon's worship. He is portrayed as an immoral leader who, for the first time in Judges, violates major elements of the covenant: intertribal violence, idolatry, and foreign sexual relations. Each has severe and lasting consequences on the nation, especially the last, as it gives rise to Abimelech and his terrible rule. It is argued that the composition of this section means to portray Gideon as disobedient and self-centered.

7:15–25

> 15And it came to pass when Gideon heard the recounting of the dream and its interpretation, that he worshipped,[54] and he returned to Israel's camp and said, "Rise! The Lord has given into your hand the camp of Midian!" 16He divided the three hundred men into three companies and put into the hands of each of them horns, empty water jars, and torches within the jars. 17And he said to them, "As you have seen with me so you should do. Behold, I am going to the edge of the camp and it shall be that as I do, so you should do. 18When I blow the horn, me

---

54. Whereas the Masoretic text provides no direct object, the Septuagint adds κυρίῳ ("Lord"). Many commentators side with the former and do not include κυρίῳ. See Gray, *Joshua*, 293; Moore, *Judges*, 211; Boling, *Judges*,147–48; Soggin, *Judges*, 143–44. Instead, they tend to change the nuance of the English verb to avoid the need for an object, rendering it "prostrated himself" (Moore, 206) "did obeisance" (Gray, 293), "knelt" (Soggin, 140). Soggin (141) has suggested the presence of the object κυρίῳ in the LXX is due to the verb προσκυνέω ("to prostrate, worship"), which in the present context needs further clarification. Such an idea is consonant with general principles of textual criticism and would best explain the variance. See Jobes and Silva, *Invitation*, 154–55. Therefore, the Masoretic wording should be preserved. It is also argued that "worshiped" should be retained as the English translation, since it best communicates the Hebrew connotation (and does not demand a direct object) and maintains the intended literary ambiguity.

75

and all those with me, you yourselves shall also blow the horns around all the camp and say, "For the Lord and for Gideon!"[55] 19So Gideon and a hundred men[56] with him went to the edge of the camp at the beginning of the middle watch, having just changed guard, and they blew the horns and shattered the jars in their hands.[57] 20And the three companies blew the horns, shattered the jars, and they grasped in their left hands the torches and in their right hands the horns to blow, and called out, "A sword for the Lord and for Gideon!" 21Each man stood in his place surrounding the camp, and all the camp ran;[58] they shouted and they put them to flight.[59] 22And they blew the three hundred horns, and the Lord set every man's sword against his fellow and the whole camp, and the camp fled until Beth-Shittah toward Zererah, until the border of Abel-Meholah by Tabbath. 23And the men of

---

55. In a few Hebrew manuscripts, the SeptuagintRlIIC, Syriac versions, and Targumim, "a sword" appears at the beginning of this verse ("A sword for the Lord and for Gideon!"), probably trying to harmonize with v. 20. The addition is possible and would not make a great difference. However, other parts of the phrase are slightly different in v. 20, so such harmonization is not required.

56. It is proposed by the BHS that the indefinite איש be changed to the definite האיש. Compare with 8:14.

57. SeptuagintlI renders this phrase in the singular: "and he blew the horn and shattered the jar in his hand."

58. There is a difficulty in this verse regarding the wording, whose meaning is plain enough, though peculiar. Cairo Genizah manuscripts suggest replacing "camp" with "people," apparently due to the strange idea of a camp fleeing. Scholars have also struggled with this. See Moore, *Judges*, 211; Boling, *Judges*, 147-48; Soggin, *Judges*, 143-44. It is commonly preferred to replace רוץ ("to flee") with יקץ ("to awake"). However, Soggin points out that textual evidence does not support such a change. He instead suggests that the original wording can in fact work, especially if רוץ is understood to mean "to jump up."

59. See Soggin, *Judges*, 144. Versions offer the Qere, which has וינוסו ("and they fled"). The Ketiv has the anomalous ויניסו ("and they put them to flight"). Either creates difficulties. The Qere seems best, but does not fit as well with the preceding verb ויריעו, which in the Hiphil usually indicates a war cry or an acclamation in a religious or political sense. This would require that the Israelites be the subject of ויריעו, for the Midianites' cry is one of fear. Therefore, it may be best to accept the rare use of ויניסו ("and they put them to flight").

Israel were mustered,[60] from Naphtali, Asher, and from all of Manasseh, and they pursued Midian. 24And Gideon sent messengers into all the hill country of Ephraim, saying, "Come down against Midian, and take the waters up to Beth-Barah and the Jordan." So all the men of Ephraim were gathered, and they captured the waters up to Beth-Barah and the Jordan. 25And they captured the two princes of Midian, Oreb and Zeeb, and they killed Oreb at the rock of Orev and Zeeb at the winepress of Zeeb. They pursued[61] Midian, and the heads of Oreb and Zeeb they brought to Gideon from across the Jordan.

This section begins with 7:15, the turning point, and transitions into the latter half of the story. Here the plot tension occupying the first half (6:1—7:15a), that of doubt versus belief, is resolved, and a new one arises, the immorality of Gideon. It has been argued that the pivotal event that links these two plot tensions and provides their transition is Gideon's act of worship. Of primary importance here is how the text works to emphasize this act of worship and how its constituent parts lead the reader to both question the nature of Gideon's worship and interpret the ensuing events in new light.

The word used in 7:15 for worship, חוה, is common in the Old Testament. Strictly speaking, it refers to the physical act of prostrating oneself,[62] usually before a higher human authority, other gods, or Yahweh himself. It is commonly thought that this act also reveals an inner attitude of submission toward the object of worship. In Deuteronomy, which serves as a foundation for the rest of the Deuteronomistic writings, the association with inner attitude is especially clear. Strong evidence for this connection in Deuteronomy is the pairing of חוה ("to worship") and עבד ("to serve"), for

---

60. See Soggin, *Judges*, 129. The Septuagint has an active form of צעק ("to muster"), compared to the passive (Niphal) in the Masoretic text. In the Septuagint's view, Gideon would be the subject. There is no convincing reason to consider this, however.

61. The Septuagint, Syriac, and Vulgate have את (direct object marker) instead of אל ("to"). This is reasonable, since אל would make little sense here.

62. Preuss, "חוה," 249–56.

Puzzling Portraits

example, 4:19 and 17:3.[63] The two words appear paired together to form one catchphrase, one cumulative idea of worship.[64] The connotation is that outward action represents inner disposition. For example, Deuteronomy 8:19 warns against the punishment for idolatry: "If you ever forget the Lord your God and follow other gods and serve (עבד) and bow down (חוה) to them, I testify against you today that you will surely be destroyed." The idea is that prostration (חוה) is not just hollow, outward action, but is representative of inner attitudes, which ultimately manifest in serving (עבד) the object worshiped. Worship of any object other than Yahweh results in deviance from his ways (1 Kings 9:6; 2 Chronicles 7:19).

What is interesting in 7:15 is that חוה has no object. Most would assume it refers to Yahweh,[65] and translations such as the NIV even supply "God," but in the Hebrew text there is no explicit object given: ויהי כשמע גדעון את־מספר החלום ואת־שברו וישתחו ("It came to pass that when Gideon heard the dream and its interpretation, he worshiped."). Yahweh is in fact never the object of this verb in Judges. All its other occurrences are in the introduction, where the objects are always foreign gods.[66] That is, they chronicle idolatrous worship. So, at the very least, it should be noted that Judges does not set a precedent for Yahweh being the object of חוה.

Further, it seems that the purpose of the omission of "Yahweh" is to create ambiguity about Gideon's worship. Wolfgang Bluedorn has noticed this dynamic and proposes the intent is to emphasize Gideon's self-centeredness.[67] That is, the ambiguity aims to show that Gideon does not in fact worship Yahweh wholly, but also himself. Bluedorn finds evidence for this in the 7:18, when Gideon instructs the men to shout "for Gideon and for the Lord!"

---

63. Ibid., 255. In fact, in Deuteronomy חוה nearly always appears paired with עבד (in every occurrence save two: 4:19 and 26:10).

64. Ibid., 254.

65. Block, *Judges*, 280; Boling, *Judges*, 143; Klein, *Triumph*, 57; Soggin, *Judges*, 140–41; Younger, *Judges*, 190–91.

66. It only occurs in 2:12, 17, 19, and 7:15.

67. Bluedorn, *Yahweh*, 136–38. It is noteworthy that outside of Bluedorn's work, one searches in vain for critical reflection on the omission of "Yahweh" and its theological significance in this passage.

Gideon wants the credit and the glory for victory, though Yahweh has emphasized that he alone deserves the accolade.

Though Bluedorn's assertion is true, it needs to be nuanced. In addition to the idea that Gideon is self-centered (worshiping himself), it also seems that the ambiguity is meant to raise the question, Whom else is Gideon worshiping?[68] The implied answer is Baal. Gideon is worshiping Baal, the god of the Canaanites. As the narrative progresses, the reader is gradually exposed to elements that confirm this conclusion. Gideon displays behavior consonant with a worshiper of Baal. Evidence supporting this claim comes from several areas: the theme of the book of Judges; the motifs in the Gideon account; and elements of characterization. The specific elements of characterization will be discussed as they arise in later scenes.

It has been said already that the theme of Judges is the Canaanization of Israel. As the book progresses, the reader is led to conclude that Israel's disobedience to Yahweh is shaping her into the likeness of the very nation she was to eschew: Canaan. The behavior of Israel did not corrupt suddenly and noticeably, but in gradual increments. Canaanite ideas and beliefs filtered into the society so discretely that most people probably did not even realize their origin. They became associated with Yahwism as time passed. This, too, was probably the case with Gideon. He came to hold a variety of ideas about what he considered true Yahwistic piety. Thus, part of Gideon's problematic worship was his native beliefs, imbued by his family and culture.

The description of Gideon's father lends credence to this idea. In 6:25–26, the Lord commands Gideon to tear down his father's altar to Baal and its accompanying Asherah pole.[69] The implication

---

68. Such a question seems natural, since it has been demonstrated that the tendency is to fill in the gap with a name (Yahweh).

69. See Schneider, *Judges*, 100. Schneider suggests that "the evil" (Judg 6:1) committed by the Israelites, the exact nature of which is unspecified by the text, may refer to intermarriage with foreigners that leads to idolatrous worship. She believes the description of Gideon's father, Joash, betrays the results of foreign relationships. Though it is hard to be certain, it is at least plausible that intermarriage with foreigners is the underlying issue giving rise

is that Gideon's father was a Baalist, who provided a worship site for the community. It cannot be known for sure exactly what this means for Gideon's upbringing, but it may be assumed that he was strongly influenced by Baalist notions of deity. His notions of God were probably an amalgamation of Baalist and Yahwist religions.[70] More will be said about this later, but here it should be noted that non-Yahwistic beliefs are evident in the way Gideon tests Yahweh (6:36–40), his making and use of the ephod (7:25–27), and his liaison with the Shechemite woman (8:31). In sum, it seems Gideon was influenced by the Baalistic ideas prevalent in his family and community.

The Jerub-Baal/Gideon name motif further strengthens the notion that Gideon displayed Baalistic tendencies. The name by which the character is first known is גדעון ("Gideon"), and ירבעל ("Jerub-Baal") is the name given to him by his father during the incident of Baal's altar. Either name is used throughout the rest of the narrative.[71] Much has been written about the origin and function of the name "Jerub-Baal."[72] What is important for this discussion, however, is the explanation given by the text. Gideon's father, Joash, answers the angry townspeople, saying "If Baal truly is a god, he can defend himself," and the narrator summarizes the scene, "So that day they called Gideon 'Jerub-Baal,' saying, 'Let Baal contend with him,' because he broke down Baal's altar" (6:31–2). Thus the text understands "Jerub-Baal" to mean "let Baal contend."

The irony in this meaning is that Baal does indeed contend.[73] At the time of the naming, "Jerub-Baal" is an insult to Baal, whose

---

to idolatrous living like that of Joash.

70. One can assume at least some substance of Yahwistic belief from what Gideon said in his response to the angel in 6:13, concerning the Exodus tradition.

71. ירבעל ("Jerub-Baal") appears only four times in the Gideon account (6:32; 7:1; 8:29, 35), and גדעון ("Gideon") the rest of the times.

72. For a good summary of the issues, see Bluedorn, *Yahweh*, 101–6.

73. See Klein, *Triumph*, 67–68. It should be noted that Klein's expression of the idea is somewhat different than mine. She suggests that the irony with the name "Jerub-Baal" is that Gideon himself contends with Yahweh. Through his wrongful behavior, Gideon the judge becomes the greatest contender *against* Yahwism.

alter lay in ruins. However, as the story progresses, it is Gideon, the so-called Yahwist, whose life turns to ruin. Accordingly, the name takes on new irony, for Baal seems to be winning the challenge, as Gideon ends his life looking as much like a Baalist as a Yahwist. Beyond Gideon's life is that of his son Abimelech, whose conception resulted from a sinful foreign liaison and whose reign wreaked havoc on Israel. Abimelech stands as condemnation of Gideon's sin. What is interesting about the Abimelech account is that in it Gideon is only referred to as "Jerub- Baal." It may be assumed, then, that the exclusive use of "Jerub-Baal" implies that Baal has indeed contended and is winning. Therefore, Gideon's Baalist beliefs are manifesting themselves fully in the life of his son Abimelech.[74] The significance of the name motif in the Gideon and Abimelech accounts is that it strengthens the idea that Gideon is associated with Baalist qualities.

The next verses (7:16–18) deal with preparation for battle and the conquering of the Midianites. What is significant here is the way in which the battle is handled. Though some tactics are common military fare, most are not. To arm an army with horns, jars, and torches is not common practice, which is exactly the point. As made clear in 7:2, Yahweh aims to conquer Midian in such a way that the Israelites cannot boast. Yahweh's first measure is to reduce Gideon's army to three hundred men, an incredibly small number for warring. His second measure, apparently, is to have Gideon arm the men with bizarre items, items that would clearly put them at a disadvantage. These elements set the stage for Yahweh's victory, so it is no surprise that Midian is conquered without the men doing any fighting. All they do is smash the jars and blow the horns, and Yahweh causes the Midianites to turn against themselves. Gideon's battle cry also should be noted: "For Yahweh and for Gideon!"[75] This will be discussed more later. For now, it is enough to highlight the stark contrast between Yahweh's express desire that he alone

74. See Block, *Judges*, 302–3.
75. Younger, *Judges*, 190–91. Younger suggests that, in light of an inscription discovered at Ekron, Gideon's victory cry may have a subtle royal allusion, foreshadowing his own kingly ambitions.

Puzzling Portraits

get credit for victory, and Gideon's inclusion of his own name in the victory cry.[76]

This scene ends with an account of Midian's routing (7:19–25). In line with the theme that the victory is Yahweh's alone, the rhetorical style of these verses is summative. They quickly move through the ensuing events, chronicling what went on but giving no emphasis. The narrator records how far the survivors fled and that the tribes of Naphtali, Asher, Manasseh, and eventually Ephraim were called out to aid in the routing. There are also the details of the capture of Oreb and Zeeb, Midian's princes, and how they were killed. Literarily, these verses give the feeling that this routing is the Israelites' formalizing of what God has already accomplished.

8:1–3

> 1 Then the men[77] of Ephraim said to him, "What is this thing you have done to us? Before calling to us you went to fight the Midianites!" And they strived with him strongly. 2 And he said to them, "What have I done now in comparison with you? Are not the gleanings of Ephraim better than the vintage of Abiezer?" 3 Into your hand God[78] has given Orev and Zeeb, the chieftains of Midian. And what have I been able to do in comparison to you?" Then their hostility subsided from against him when he spoke this thing.

---

76. Schneider, *Judges*, 115. Schneider suggests another way that the text emphasizes Gideon's wrongful appropriation of credit for the victory: by drawing a contrast with the Deborah episode (Judges 4–5). When Gideon sequesters acclaim for Yahweh's victory, it is meant to stand in stark relief to Deborah's behavior: the lengthy song of praise to the Lord for his deliverance (ch. 5).

77. The BHS has the singular איש ("man"), and the SeptuagintAO and Latin versions have a singular verb to match ויאמר ("and he said").

78. Against the Masoretic reading of אלהים, the Septuagint and Vulgate have יהוה, which is followed at times (e.g., Boling, *Judges*, 150). However, recently it has been asserted that the use of אלהים may be purposeful and serve a rhetorical function. See Block, *Judges*, 286.

The aim of this scene is twofold: (1) to emphasize the growing issue of tribal disunity and (2) to cast ambiguity on Gideon's character.[79] In Judges, tribal issues tend to be portrayed with an emphasis both on how the tribal issue arises and on how the leader handles it. Here the root of the tribal issue—Ephraim's discontent—is shown in a negative light, while the way in which Gideon handles it is portrayed positively. Curiously, Gideon's careful and diplomatic handling of Ephraim's anger becomes the very thing that condemns him later, when he instead chooses to brutalize his own people. More will be said about that in the appropriate passage. Also, though this scene does not explicitly condemn Gideon, it does in fact cast an ambiguous light on his character, an aspect that will be further developed as the story progresses.

It is not exactly clear why Ephraim was so displeased with its lot in the Midianite conflict. What is clear is that Ephraim is portrayed as contentious and quarreling.[80] A similar situation involving Ephraim is recorded in 12:1–6, which seems to invite the same implications. The point, then, is to show that Ephraim is a divisive group that is rarely content with its lot in life. Of course, this individual example of Ephraim is representative of the larger problems within Israel.

Another emphasis of the scene is Gideon's answer to Ephraim. Gideon clearly handles the situation with skill and tact. However, other issues are not so clear. On the one hand, it is not certain how the reader should morally evaluate Gideon's answer. Is his answer good, an example of quick, careful thinking, or is it bad, an example of calculated manipulation? The presence of peculiarities may lead the reader to see it as bad.[81] For one thing, although Gideon received his instructions from the Lord, he says nothing of them in responding to Ephraim. It seems his greatest defense would be rooted in Yahweh's command. Second, Gideon's answer instead

---

79. See O'Connell, *Rhetoric*, 154–55. Though O'Connell identifies a different plot dynamic overall, he agrees that the two concerns in this scene are tribal disunity and Gideon's corroding character.

80. See Block, *Judges*, 284.

81. Ibid., 286. See also Younger, *Judges*, 197.

Puzzling Portraits

appeals to the self-centered sensibilities of Ephraim. He says nothing about the situation at hand but only speaks about Ephraim's accomplishments, apparently to flatter them.[82] In brief, Gideon's answer is psychologically, not theologically, based.[83] And third, in naming God, Gideon uses אלהים not יהוה. This raises questions, for it seems to echo two incidents in which אלהים was used: Gideon's fleece testings (6:36–40) and the words of the Midianite soldier interpreting the dream (7:14).[84] The significance is that Gideon's words here betray his lack of understanding. Was it God generally or Yahweh specifically who delivered Israel? In these ways, Gideon is shown to have ambiguous moral character, a trait that will arise in later scenes.

8:4–21

4Then Gideon went to the Jordan and crossed over[85] it, and with him were three hundred men who were weary[86] but who were (still) pursuing. 5And he said to the men of Succoth, "Please give loaves of bread to the people who are following me, for they are weary and I am pursuing Zebah and Zalmunna, kings of Midian." 6And the chieftains of Succoth said,[87] "Are the hands of Zebah and Zalmunna now in your hand,[88] that bread should be given to your army?" 7Gideon said, "So be it, when the Lord gives Zebah and Zalmunna into my hand, I shall thresh your flesh with the thorns of the desert and with

---

82. Klein, *Triumph*, 60–61.
83. Block, *Judges*, 286.
84. Bluedorn, *Yahweh*, 151.
85. The Septuagint, Syriac, and Vulgate render it as an aorist, which the BHS suggests should be read, ויעברהו ("and he crossed over it"), rather than as a participle. Most translators follow suit. See Soggin, *Judges*, 149.
86. The Septuagint adds "and hungry."
87. BHS suggests reading with Hebrew manuscripts, Sebir, and versions, which use a plural verbal form. This translation is adopted here.
88. A few Hebrew manuscripts and some Versions (Syriac and Arabic) change "your hand" to the plural "your hands."

Judges 7:15—8:33

the briars."⁸⁹ 8Then he went up from there to Penuel and spoke like this, and the men of Penuel answered him like the men of Succoth did. 9And he spoke also to the men of Penuel, saying "When I return in peace I will pull down this tower!" 10Now Zebah and Zalmunna were in Karkor, and their camp with them, 15,000, all those who were left over from the camp of the sons of the east; and those who had fallen were 120,000, men who drew a sword (swordsmen). 11And Gideon went up by way of those who live⁹⁰ in tents⁹¹ of the east to Nobah and Jogbehah, and he struck the camp when the camp was in safety.⁹² 12And Zebah and Zalmunna escaped⁹³ and he pursued after them and captured the two kings of Midian, Zebah and Zalmunna; and he routed⁹⁴ the camp in terror. 13And Gideon son of Joash returned from the battle by the ascent of Heres.⁹⁵ 14And he captured a young man from the men of Succoth and questioned him, and he wrote down for him the chieftains of Succoth and its elders, seventy-seven men. 15And he went to the men⁹⁶ of Succoth and said, "Behold! Zebah and Zalmunna about whom you reproached me saying, 'Are the hands of Zebah and Zalmunna already in your hand, that we should give bread to your men who are weary?'" 16So he took the elders of the city, and with thornbushes

---

89. BHS offers a reading that exchanges את for the preposition ב before "thorns" and "briars."

90. BHS suggests שוכני instead of השכוני.

91. An unusual construct chain which has within it a preposition (ב). See Boling, *Judges*, 156.

92. A few Hebrew manuscripts and the Septuagint have the participial form בטח. It would not change the meaning significantly.

93. Codex Leningrad, several Hebrew manuscripts (Edd), Cairo Codex of the Hebrew Prophets, and the Edition of Bombergiana Iacobi ben Chajjim (Venetiis 1524/5) have the defective reading: וינסו.

94. The SeptuagintA and Josephus offer a stronger word than החריד ("to route"): הכחיד ("to annihilate"). There is no substantial reason to accept this view. Soggin, *Judges*, 151.

95. Following the Septuagint, BHS suggests that the prefixed ל be replaced with a מ, which would read, ממעלה. The translation above has adopted this idea.

96. The Septuagint has "the chieftains" instead of "men."

of the desert and briars he taught[97] the men of Succoth a lesson. 17And the tower of Penuel he pulled down, and he killed the men of the city. 18And he said to Zebah and Zalmunna, "Of what kind were the men whom you killed in Tabor? And they answered, "Their likeness and yours are the same—like the appearance of the sons of a king."[98] 19And he said, "They were my brothers, the sons of my mother. As surely as the Lord lives, if you would have let them live I would not kill you." 20And he said to Jether his first-born, "Rise, kill them!" But the boy would not draw his sword, for he was afraid because he was still a youth. 21Then Zebah and Zalmunna said, "You rise and fall upon us, for as is a man, so is his might."[99] So Gideon rose and killed Zebah and Zalmunna, and he took the crescent things (ornaments), which were around the necks of their camels.

This section, composed of three scenes (8:4–9, 10–14, 15–21), is an important piece in the development of the Gideon story. It features two larger emphases: Gideon's poor character and tribal disunity. What it demonstrates in particular is that these two elements are inherently connected[100] and, further, that they are also linked to the original idea of Gideon's impure beliefs. They form a cause-and-effect relationship, in which impure belief leads to poor

---

97. The Masoretic text reads ידע ("he taught"), whereas many ancient textual witnesses (Septuagint, Syriac, Vulgate) have ידש ("he threshed"). Many scholars prefer the latter reading, for it seems to make the most sense in context. However, the MT reading has been retained here on the principle that the most difficult reading is often correct. See the English Standard Version for a modern Bible translation that keeps the MT rendering.

98. The uniqueness of this phrase has caused wonderment. As it stands, it literally means, "one is your likeness, their likeness." The Targumim and Vulgate render it אחד אחד ("each one"), whereas some Hebrew manuscripts, Codex Veronensis, Theodotian, and the Syriac omit אחד altogether. Commentators tend to not comment (Boling, Soggin), though Moore suggests amending to כל אחד ("all one"). Regardless, the translation would be similar: "your likeness and theirs is the same." See Moore, *Judges*, 228.

99. The SeptuagintBC2 suggests changing "his might" to "your might." However, this appears to be a popular proverb, and thus should remain as the Masoretic text has it. See Soggin, *Judges*, 155.

100. See O'Connell, *Rhetoric*, 150–53.

character, and poor character leads to poor behavior, and poor behavior leads to tribal disunity. Rhetorically, this section accomplishes its goals by using two main literary devices: psychological characterization and a "hand" motif. Two main encounters are featured here, one between Gideon and the leaders of Succoth and Penuel (vv. 4–9, 14–17), and the other between him and the kings of Midian (vv. 18–21). For each, the literary devices work similarly, though they reveal different aspects of Gideon's character.

Psychological characterization refers to the portrayal of a character's inner life, including thoughts, emotions, and motivations. It does not necessarily differ from other sorts of characterization, other than it focuses on the inner person. The reason it is important to the Gideon cycle is because, more than other stories in Judges, it undergirds the plotline and is at work throughout.[101] For example, in the first half of the story the main tension is Gideon's struggle to believe Yahweh. The root of this problem is Gideon's emotion (fear). In the same way, the second half features Gideon's immoral behavior. The root of it, it was suggested, is Gideon's belief (albeit impure belief). Specifically, such character study is important in this section because it reveals the underlying motivations for Gideon's actions, which lead to both unwarranted brutality and tribal disunity.

In the encounter with the leaders of Succoth and Penuel, it is not clear how the situation should have unfolded. However, it can be assumed, on the one hand, that the leaders should have given aid to Gideon and his men,[102] and on the other, that Gideon's reaction was too harsh.[103] Regarding his reaction, in at least two ways the text emphasizes aspects of his character through psychological characterization. First is the fact that this event follows closely after Gideon's encounter with the Ephraimites, in which he is shown to

---

101. See Assis, *Self-Interest*, 126–27.

102. See Block, *Judges*, 290. Block argues that the use of שרים ("chieftains") and מגדל ("tower") in talking about the two towns probably indicates they were military outposts. This would lend even more credence to the idea that they should have helped Gideon and his army.

103. That Succoth and Penuel were both Israelite towns, see respectively, Seely "Succoth," 217–18, and Slayton "Penuel," 223.

Puzzling Portraits

be quite capable of navigating confrontations. Gideon's diplomatic response stands in stark contrast to this brutal one. The question arises as to why Gideon acts so harshly here. Second, the text highlights that the reason for Gideon's behavior was rage. Gideon was treated poorly, and he repaid that treatment with wrath. In fact, Gideon's own vows confirm that he acted out of anger.

Gideon's use of the name Yahweh confirms the problem with his character. In the last chapter, it was discussed how biblical narrative reveals inner dispositions by contrasting narrative and dialogue. One way of accomplishing this is by emphasizing the disparity between the narrated facts and the words of the character. In this encounter, "Yahweh" appears once (v. 7), and only in Gideon's vow against the leaders. Gideon is claiming divine sanction for his behavior.[104] The narrator himself, however, never confirms any of Gideon's words.[105] Thus a disparity arises between what Gideon claims and what the narrator records. The reader must ascertain whether Gideon is using the name of Yahweh out of ignorance or for manipulation. Either option is feasible, but the latter probably is more likely. Klein may be right that Gideon's rage is due to the people's doubt in him.[106] If this is the case, then his use of "Yahweh" surely is manipulative, for it has been shown already that Gideon disobeyed the Lord and included himself as co-victor in the battle cry. Gideon's chronic problem is being consumed with himself.[107]

The second encounter, between Gideon and the kings of Midian, further develops the flaws of Gideon's character. Since 8:12, the reader has known of the kings' capture, which was put aside to tell of Gideon's dealings with Succoth and Penuel. In verse 18, however, it comes to the fore again. The verse begins with an unusual question: "Of what kind were the men who you killed at Tabor?" The question is not exactly as it seems. It is a means to get the kings to indict themselves for killing Gideon's brothers. The

---

104. Klein, *Triumph*, 61.

105. See Webb, *Book of Judges*, 151. Webb notes that there is "no indication of any involvement by Yahweh."

106. Klein, *Triumph*, 61–62.

107. See Assis, *Self-Interest*, 121.

revelation of Gideon's driving motive introduces a new dynamic to the story, for it becomes clear that he had been pursuing these kings not for Yahweh's purposes but his own, to avenge his brothers' deaths.

At work here is a rhetorical device discussed in the last chapter: the character-elevated position. It will be recalled that the purpose of this device is to limit the reader's information about a character to create a certain effect. Often it is used to hide a character's true motivation, so that when revealed it causes the reader to reinterpret the entire story. This device is also meant to surprise and, accordingly, emphasize particular elements. In this case, the text disguises Gideon's motivation for pursuing Zebah and Zalmunna. The reader was led to believe that Gideon pursued the Midianite kings as part of Yahweh's program, his war against Israel's oppressors. However, this scene reveals that Gideon was in fact driven by a personal vendetta.[108] It was not righteous obedience, then, but rage that drove him. Gideon is not motivated by Yahwistic piety, but by selfish ambition.

A hand motif also plays an important rhetorical role in this section.[109] A motif is a repeated word or idea that functions to direct the reader to themes or emphases of the work.[110] In this passage, the English word "hand," which spans all of Judges, has special importance. Actually, there are two Hebrew words for "hand": יד and כף. In general, יד occurs more often and has a larger range of meaning, usually being used metaphorically to connote power.[111] כף tends to be used in the more literal sense of "palm," "hand," or "hollow (of the hand)."[112] In the Gideon cycle, this tendency in the meaning of כף is mostly true, though in a couple of cases כף does function metaphorically to connote power (6:13, 14).

---

108. Most commentators agree on this point: See, e.g., Block, *Judges*, 287–88; Klein, *Triumph*, 61–62; Webb, *Book of Judges*, 151. For a very different view, cf. Soggin, *Judges*, 155–56.

109. It is interesting that commentators do not discuss the hand motif.

110. See Amit, "Multi-Purpose," 109.

111. Dreytza, "יד," 402–5.

112. Dreytza, "כף," 686–87.

Puzzling Portraits

Crucial to the use of "hand" in this cycle is its connection with "to save" (ישע).[113] This combination appears often and in pivotal places, such as in Gideon's call (6:14), his instruction by Yahweh concerning the Midianites (7:2, 7), and in relation to the common phrase "sold into the hand of" (6:1, 13, etc.). The practical impact of the word combination on the story is that it draws attention to the question of whose hand does the delivering, whose hand is in control. It is clear that Yahweh is the only one whose hand is powerful to save, and any other agents, whether Midian or Gideon, are only secondary instruments.

In this section (8:4–21), the hand motif culminates. It is suggested the motif serves to emphasize that Gideon's motivation is selfish ambition, not Yahwistic obedience. Judges makes clear that no hand but Yahweh's saves. If any other claims to do so, it is an imposter. Interestingly, in verses 4–21, the narrative intensifies this play on the hand motif directly in regard to Gideon. There is a heated exchange between Gideon and the men of Succoth (v. 6). They ask if the "hand" (כף) of Zebah and Zalmunna is in Gideon's hand (יד). That is, they ask a rhetorical question about the literal hands of the kings being in Gideon's possession. Gideon responds by saying that, when the Lord gives the kings into his hand (יד), he will return in vengeance (v. 7). The irony of this exchange is that the Lord is never mentioned apart from Gideon's words.[114] It is another example of intentional contrast between Gideon's claims and the narrator's record. What seems to be implied is that Gideon has credited himself with the authority and power of Yahweh. Despite all the Lord's precautions to prevent the people from giving themselves the glory (7:2), Gideon has done exactly that. All the familiar markers of Yahweh's activity are now absent.[115] There is no mention of Yahweh's presence or of his delivering of Midian into Gideon's "hand." It is Gideon alone who "pursues" (8:12) and "falls upon" (8:21) the Midianites, though he claims that Yahweh "delivered" them into his "hand" (8:7).

---

113. Amit, *Book of Judges*, 264–65.
114. Klein, *Triumph*, 61.
115. Webb, *Book of Judges*, 151.

8:22-27

22And each man of Israel said[116] to Gideon, "Rule over us—even you, even your son, even the son of your son, for you have delivered us from the hand of Midian. 23And Gideon said to them, "I myself will not rule over you, and my son will not rule over you; the Lord will rule over you." 24Yet Gideon said to them, "Let me ask a request: Let each man give me a ring of his plunder (for they had gold rings because they were Ishmaelites). 25And they said, "We will certainly give them." And they spread[117] out a garment and each threw a ring of his plunder there. 26And it came to pass that the earrings of gold that he had requested weighed 1,700 shekels, besides the crescents and pendants and the garments of purple which were on the kings of Midian, and besides the necklaces which were on the necks of their camels. 27And Gideon made it into an ephod and he set it in his city, in Ophrah, and all of Israel whored after it there, and it became for Gideon and his family a snare.

This scene focuses on two elements: (1) Gideon's answer to the request for him to be king and (2) his making of an ephod.[118] The reading offered here suggests that these emphases serve to reveal further Gideon's immoral behavior. Again at the center of the issue is Gideon's stubborn disobedience and selfish ambition. Kingship is the issue many interpreters have focused on. However, kingship itself is not primary, but secondary (and thus subservient) to Gideon's disobedience. The discussion that follows will consider kingship, but only as it functions within the larger emphases.

---

116. A few Hebrew manuscripts, Sebir, and SeptuagintAOL have the singular form of the verb, whereas the MT has the plural.

117. The Septuagint has a singular form of the verb.

118. For a good summary of the ephod discussion, see Meyers, "Ephod," 550. Meyers makes an important point about the tension between seeing the ephod as a garment or an idol. She says that "too rigid a classification between garment and cultic objects as separate categories" has emerged. Instead, we should view the ephod according to its function not necessarily its form. For an in-depth discussion, see Bluedorn, *Yahweh*, 170-78.

Puzzling Portraits

The discussion of kingship in this passage generally revolves around several questions. Is Gideon's answer genuine? If so, does it reflect the larger ideals of Judges? Or instead, is his answer a polite way of accepting kingship? In addition to these questions, some scholars have added a more foundational one: To what does Gideon's answer refer—kingship proper or the reasons for which it comes about? Amit holds that Gideon does in fact reject human kingship. She finds convincing evidence in the ephod incident.[119] To her mind, Gideon's building of the ephod is a reaction to the people's request. On hearing the people's wrongheaded desire, he sets out to help ensure that they recognize Yahweh as true savior and king. The way in which he does this is by building the ephod, an item to serve as both a historical reminder and a cultic symbol.[120] So the ephod, though it becomes a stumbling block, was wrought of Gideon's good intentions to preserve Yahweh as king. An interesting dynamic, therefore, exists between Amit's view of this incident—the rejection of kingship—and that of the larger book of Judges, which commends kingship. She asserts that the interplay between Judges' negative and positive connotations of kingship create a realistic picture of the coming monarchy. Though the larger book commends kingly rule, it does so with realism about the perils. This passage is a genuine rejection of human kingship, and together with the following account of Abimelech develops an honest portrait of kingship. In contrast to Amit, O'Connell suggests Gideon's rejection refers not to kingship itself, but to the way in which the request for it arose.[121] That is, he believes Gideon rejects the motive behind the people's request for a king, not the institution.[122] In O'Connell's mind, there are two problems

---

119. Amit, *Book of Judges*, 260–62.

120. See Webb, *Book of Judges*, 152–53. Webb sees the ephod as a way for the people to inquire of the Lord, instead of as simply a cultic symbol. As such, Gideon's attempt with the ephod was to allow the Lord to reign as king and to present the people a means for communicating with him.

121. O'Connell, *Rhetoric*, 163–64.

122. For more on this, see Howard, "Case for Kingship." Here Howard reviews and largely sides with Gerbrandt, *Kingship*. According to Howard,

Judges 7:15—8:33

with the request. First, there is no mention of Yahweh choosing the king; it is only the people's desire. To O'Connell, any request for kingship must be rooted in Yahweh's will. Second, the people are wrong-minded in their reasons for wanting a king. Instead of wanting a king to lead them in Yahwistic piety and social issues, they want one for military deliverance. For such deliverance, however, they are supposed to trust Yahweh, not a fellow human. Thus, O'Connell ultimately finds that the passage says nothing negative about kingship itself, but only about the manner in which the request for it arose here.

Perhaps there is a better way to understand this passage as it concerns kingship. Gordon McConville has written insightfully on the canonical view of the nature of kingship.[123] He asserts that the biblical idea of kingship is not so black or white as some scholars believe. To McConville, there is a larger ideal at work, and kingship only functions as part of that. The ideal is the rule of Israel by Yahweh's Torah.[124] That is, Yahweh's primary concern was to establish a society characterized by obedience to Torah rule. Theoretically, such a society would form Israel into a righteous people who reflected the ways of Yahweh.[125]

McConville says provision is made for this society in Deuteronomy 16:18—18:22.[126] The fundamental element is the distribution of power. There are to be judges and officers (16:18-19), priests (18:1-8), a high court composed of these two offices (17:8-13), and prophets (18:15-22). Together these offices serve to evenly distribute the ruling power of Israel. What is especially in-

---

Gerbrandt's main thrust is that in contrast to traditional opinion, Deuteronomy through Kings has a positive view of the monarchy. The seemingly negative opinion that emerges concerns the manner of kingship, not its existence. Mainly, an ideal kingship would lead the people in Yahwistic worship and maintain the covenant, while trusting the Lord to fight its battles. The biblical material, then, shows Israel's sin being their desire for a king with reversed priorities, especially concerning warfare and only partly concerning faith.

123. McConville, "Law," 69-88.
124. Ibid., 77.
125. Ibid., 79-80.
126. Ibid., 76-77.

teresting is that these offices are mandated, while the office of king is permitted.[127] The king was not necessary, nor even ideal, in the governing structure of Israel. Apparently, the presence of a king was a result of Yahweh's accommodation to Israel's stubborn insistence.[128] In the event that a king should come to power, however, he was to be different than those of the rest of the ancient Near East. Deuteronomy 17:14-20 lays out the stipulations. The king is to meet four requirements in particular: he is to be (1) appointed by Yahweh (v. 15); (2) a brother to the people (v. 20); (3) subservient to Torah (vv. 18-20); and (4) he shall not hoard possessions or take many wives (vv. 16-17). The practical function of the stipulations was to maintain dispersed authority and Torah rule.

It is clear, in McConville's opinion, that the Bible does not have one ideal model for Israel's political structure.[129] The important part was the purpose: Israel ruled by Torah and shaped into a righteous people that reflected Yahweh's character. Certain political structures were deemed better than others for the task, which is why kingship at times received negative treatment. Due to its nature, kingship would make difficult the realization of God's desires for his people,[130] for it tended to corrupt the distribution of power and compromise the authority of Torah. It may be concluded, therefore, that McConville does not think the canonical witness views kingship as unequivocally evil, but instead, as something that, if used properly, may yield positive results. The problem is that kingship's nature does not bode well for producing societal and moral gain.

McConville's ideas have important implications for this study. They reveal that the primary theological issue is not merely with the office of king, but with the rule of Yahweh and the formation of his people. Accordingly, each occurrence that deals with kingship should be interpreted in this light. Regarding Judges 8:22-23, it should be asked how Gideon's behavior compares to the ideals

127. Ibid., 77.
128. Ibid., 75.
129. Ibid., 84.
130. Ibid., 83.

set out in Deuteronomy 17:14-20. Immediately obvious is the fact that the comparison portrays Gideon negatively. He is not appointed by Yahweh, deals treacherously with his countrymen, takes a foreign concubine, and gathers precious materials to make an ephod, which leads him and all Israel astray.

Block is right that the text accomplishes its message by contrasting Gideon's words and deeds.[131] However, more should be said about the process of comparison in this particular scene. It will be remembered from the last chapter that a device called opposition in juxtaposition is often employed in biblical narrative. Two contrasting events are placed side by side in a story to highlight a certain incongruity. The nature of the incongruity is the emphasis of that passage, often revealing a character's motives and priorities. This scene places in opposition verses 22 (Gideon's refusal of kingship) and 23 (Gideon's making of the ephod).

The incongruity that results is as follows. Gideon refuses to be king, but he immediately acts in a manner characteristic of kingship. Block argues that a number of elements are meant to echo royal rule.[132] Several of his observations are convincing: Gideon's gathering of gold from dead enemies and the collecting of royal symbols from the kings and their camels (vv. 24-26); his making of the ephod and establishing it in his home town Ophrah (v. 27); and his taking of many wives and a foreign concubine (vv. 31-32). These elements strongly suggest royal behavior on the part of Gideon.

The implication is that Gideon was disobedient. It is assumed that Gideon's refusal of kingship was based on common knowledge of kingship's undesirability.[133] His comment reveals a personal understanding of Yahweh's ultimate desires. However, Gideon's ensuing behavior betrays his own inner attitudes and ambitions. Contra Amit, many scholars have interpreted the ephod incident

---

131. Block, *Judges*, 298-99.
132. Ibid., 298-301.
133. See Block, *Judges*, 298; Bluedorn, *Yahweh*, 170; Boling, *Judges*, 160; Klein, *Triumph*, 64; Schneider, *Judges*, 127; Soggin, *Judges*, 160; Webb, *Book of Judges*, 152.

as proof of Gideon's wrongful ambitions.[134] Klein's position is most likely in view of the context. She suggests that the ephod, probably too heavy to be a garment, is a golden object of worship established by Gideon to commemorate his own achievements.[135] This idea would fit well in the context of the Gideon story: Gideon has already included himself in Yahweh's victory cry (7:18) and failed to correct the people's belief that he, not Yahweh, delivered them from Midian (8:22). Therefore, the resultant portrait of Gideon is that he was driven by an ambition to be recognized and lauded. That motive caused him to erect a cultic object in his hometown, something that led him, his family, and all Israel into dire idolatry (8:27).

In conclusion, the canonical idea of kingship typically has been misunderstood and, therefore, needs reconsideration. McConville provides the basis for this reconsideration. His view is that kingship is not the primary canonical issue. The true issue, the one upon which kingship rests, is the establishment of a society in which the people are obedient to and reflective of Yahweh and subservient to Torah. The problem with kingship is that it does not lend itself to these ends. Instead, it tends to corrupt societal power distribution and compromise Torah rule. This fact does not make kingship necessarily evil, but at least risky and perhaps perilous. These conclusions on kingship are proven true in Judges 8:22–27. Gideon, by way of behaving kingly, causes great harm to the Israelite people. The very thing Deuteronomy 17:14–20 is trying to avoid is realized in Gideon's rule. Particularly, there is a great contrast between Gideon's construction of the ephod and its subsequent idolatry, and the notion of an ideal king who would study Torah and lead the nation in Yahweh's ways.

---

134. See Block, *Judges*, 300–301; Bluedorn, *Yahweh*, 174; Klein, *Triumph*, 65.

135. Klein, *Triumph*, 65.

8:28-35

28And Midian was subdued before the sons of Israel, and they did not lift up their heads; and the land was quiet forty years in the days of Gideon. 29And Jerubbaal son of Joash went and dwelled in his house. 30And Gideon had seventy sons who came from his own loin, for he had many wives. 31And his concubine who was in Shechem also bore to him a son, and he appointed his name "Abimelech." 32And Gideon son of Joash died at a good old age and was buried in the grave of Joash his father, in Ophrah of the Abiezrites. 33Now it came about when Gideon had died that the sons of Israel turned back and prostituted after the Baals, and they appointed for themselves Baal-berit as God. 34And the sons of Israel did not remember the Lord their God, who delivered them from the hand of all their enemies from every side. 35And they did not show loving-kindness to the house of Jerubaal (that is, Gideon) according to all the good that he did to Israel.

This is the last scene in the Gideon story, and it holds a unique rhetorical place. On the one hand, it follows Judges' summary convention, recording the subduing of foreign enemies, a period of rest for the land, length of reign, death and place of burial of judge, and the ensuing apostasy.[136] It concludes Gideon's life similarly to other judges. On the other hand, the scene also introduces new plot tensions that form the foundation of the Abimelech account.[137] That is, this scene does not just tie up loose ends; it also introduces crucial narrative information, which provides an impetus for and transition to the following Abimelech story. What is crucial to note

---

136. On Baal-Berith, see Lewis, "Identity," 401-23. He asserts that this deity should be identified as El Berith, mentioned in 9:46. The unique naming here, he claims, is an epithet playing on the context, which deals with the ideas of covenant (unfaithfulness) and Baals.

137. The best discussion of how this works is O'Connell, *Rhetoric*, 139-71. Although this study does not follow O'Connell exactly, it is recognized that he has illumined a great many subtle dynamics of interrelation between the Gideon and Abimelech stories.

is the connection between Gideon's behavior and the ensuing narrative: Abimelech is the product of Gideon's sinful liaisons with a foreign (Shechemite) woman.[138] Abimelech's awful life and reign are seen as products of Gideon's sin and, as such, stand in condemnation of it. The thrust of this passage is to reveal the connection between Gideon's sin and the distress that Abimelech causes Israel.

In the previous scene (8:22–27), it was suggested that Gideon's verbal refusal of kingship sharply contrasted with his behavior, which did resemble kingly living. The contrast revealed Gideon's hypocritical character. This scene continues the contrast by revealing Gideon's foreign liaison and its subsequent product, Abimelech. The reading offered here suggests that these two elements in particular are meant to highlight Gideon's royal behavior and the destruction that ensues.

It has been noted that Gideon's behavior contrasts the ideals of kingship in Deuteronomy 17:17. Judges 8:22–27 echoed the latter half of verse 17 (the gathering of gold), and this scene (8:28–35) echoes the former half (the taking of many wives). Deuteronomy's prohibition against taking many wives is understood to refer to harem building.[139] A royal harem typically served the purpose of increasing a king's power base, by creating foreign alliances.[140] Though not mentioned explicitly in Deuteronomy 17:17, the prohibition also may be understood to encompass the acquiring of foreign concubines.[141] The point of the prohibition is to preserve the unique nature of Israelite society, especially the maintenance of the covenant. Implicit in this is that harem building would bring foreign women with all their attendant ideologies and social values into Israel, which would ultimately lead the nation astray.

---

138. For a good discussion on the meaning of the term פילגש ("concubine"), see Schneider, *Judges*, 128–30.

139. See Craigie, *Book of Deuteronomy*, 255–6; Merrill, *Deuteronomy*, 265; and McConville, *Deuteronomy*, 294–95.

140. McConville, *Deuteronomy*, 294.

141. Ibid., 295. See also Craigie, *Book of Deuteronomy*, 178–79. Craigie argues the underlying idea is to guard against any kind of foreign alliance that might compromise the covenant.

Judges 8:30 highlights Gideon's harem building. It does not give specific numbers but records that Gideon had "many" wives. He also had at least one foreign concubine, a Shechemite women. Gideon's liaison with this foreign woman produced a son named Abimelech[142] Abimelech would wreak havoc on the nation of Israel until Yahweh himself intervened. The consequences of Gideon's actions realize the fears of Deuteronomy 17:17. The ephod led the nation into national idolatry and covenantal apostasy. In this scene the product of the harem, Abimelech, will ultimately cause tribal brutality and disunity. Abimelech's life is characterized by violence: he slaughters all but one of his brothers (9:5) and continually wars with the men of Shechem (9:22–54). Also, his life is far from pious. The presence of God is sparse throughout the account.[143] The proper name יהוה ("Yahweh") never appears in association with Abimelech,[144] and אלהים ("God") only occurs five times (9:7, 23, 24, 56, 57), four of which record God's judgment on Abimelech (vv. 23–4, 56–7). Not once is Abimelech said to have inquired of or sought after God.[145] It may be concluded that Abimelech's life emphasizes two areas of covenant concern: tribal destruction and spiritual corruption. Ultimately, he is the "ethical and spiritual seed sown by Gideon/Jerubbaal . . . [at] full bloom and fruition."[146]

In closing, this scene (8:28–35) concludes the account of Gideon, though it does not end the consequences of his life. The passage continues the contrast between what Gideon said (rejecting kingship) and how he lived (behaving kingly). In stark relief

---

142. See Block, *Judges*, 303–4; Webb, *Book of Judges*, 154; Younger, *Judges*, 210. "Abimelech" can mean a variety of things, including "my father is king." It has been suggested that "Abimelech" may mean "my divine father is king," but in light of the context the former is probably best. Such a title would add to the cumulative portrait of Gideon's royal behavior.

143. Assis, *Self-Interest*, 139.

144. Klein, *Triumph*, 70.

145. See Polzin, *Moses*, 173–75, for a good discussion on the absence of Yahweh from Abimelech's life. Polzin argues that the phraseological phenomenon of the omission of the divine name indicates the text's ideology: Gideon's sin, manifested in Abimelech, has brought about godlessness in Israel.

146. Block, *Judges*, 308.

Puzzling Portraits

to the ideals given in Deuteronomy 17:17, Gideon did take many wives and a foreign concubine. The result, as predicted in Deuteronomy, was the corruption of the covenant society. Particularly damaged was the area of tribal solidarity. It can only be assumed that many other areas also were affected under the horrible rule of Abimelech.

CONCLUSIONS

Judges portrays Israel in a downward spiral due to covenant unfaithfulness. Its theme is the Canaanization of Israelite society. The book's purpose is to sound a prophetic call for Israel to return unto their Lord. The message of Judges is not, contra popular opinion, about kingship. Kingship does play a role, but only a subsidiary one. Following the work of McConville, it was argued that the larger ideology on which kingship stands addresses the purpose and function of Yahwistic society. Israel was meant to be a society founded on obedience to Yahweh and his Torah. There was no one right way to accomplish this task, though some were deemed better than others. Kingship was not viewed altogether favorably in this regard. However, the rule of judges did not work either.

It was suggested that the twelve judges recorded in the book played two unique rhetorical roles. On the one hand, they symbolized the people of Israel as a whole. The sins of the people were manifest in the judges. On the other hand, their personal sins contributed to the overall direction of the nation. As went the judges, so went the nation. Three literary dynamics were noted in this regard. First, the judges progressively worsened as the book developed. Second, the point at which a judge first engaged in serious covenantal disloyalty was the tipping point for the whole book. Third and last, the book's theme of Israel's struggles developed in an inclusio pattern: foreign oppression to foreign idols to domestic idols to domestic oppression. This movement is also directly tied to the judges' personal behavior.

It was argued that the Gideon account functioned as a pivot in the rhetoric of Judges. The episode was at the heart of three rhetorical dynamics already mentioned. Gideon was the first judge to engage in covenantal disloyalty (namely in tribal bloodshed), idolatrous worship, and sexual liaisons with foreign women. The move from foreign to domestic idols happened with his construction of the ephod. Abimelech, the product of Gideon's sinful liaison, incurred awful violence on Israel. It was suggested that the plotline of the Gideon story was not the Midianite conflict, as commonly held, but Gideon's struggle to believe Yahweh. The turning point, at which Gideon finally worshiped, was 7:15. However, the act of worship was highly ambiguous. Implicit in the narrative following the act of worship was Gideon's immoral behavior. That led to the conclusion that his worship was impure, being both self-centered and somewhat Baalistic (i.e., Canaanite). These tendencies were manifest in Gideon's verbal refusal of kingship, which is contrasted by his kingly behavior.

6

The Ethics of Judges 7:15—8:33

Until now this study has dealt largely with theory. Here the theory, along with exegetical findings, is applied to a specific text: Judges 7:15—8:33. Three parts shape the chapter: Ethics in Judges, Virtue and Vice, and Gideon and the Good Life. The first section deals with the unique problem of approaching the ethics of a negative book. The second addresses an important issue of the first section: the relationship between virtue and vice. The third section applies these findings to the actual text. What is argued is that to interpret the ethics of a negative book, one must focus on identifying the character's vices and discern how they corrode the goal of godly living.

ETHICS IN JUDGES

The primary question for Judges is how to understand the ethics of a generally negative book.[1] How might a work like Judges, full of failure and catastrophe, be of any value to one's moral life? The suggestion of this chapter is that negative biblical books should be used in a way similar to positive books. Perhaps the only significant

---

1. See Wenham, *Story*, 45.

difference is in the role of vices in interpretation. Whereas with positive books readers tend to look for characters' virtues, in negative ones they ought to look for vices. Specifically, it is important to understand the presence of the vices within the larger plotline: what are their causes and effects? How do these vices impair one's attainment of the good life?

It was said previously that to understand narrative ethically one must begin with an idea of "the good." This is difficult to define. What is more concrete and observable is the good life, the incarnation of the good. According to the Old Testament, the good life is characterized by blessing (good harvests, progeny, etc.), peace, and the presence of God. It also was noted that the way in which such a life is achieved is through the presence and practice of the virtues. These virtues, generally speaking, include piety, courage, generosity, mercy, loyalty, eloquence, temperance, and justice. In the Old Testament, the virtuous person is the one who is characterized by these virtues and who enjoys a life of blessing, peace, and the presence of God.

However, it was shown that the book of Judges does not often, if ever, display examples of such a good life or its virtues. Instead, it displays increasingly poor behavior and the unraveling of Israel as a nation. Judges' theme is the Canaanization of Israelite society. It was suggested that the Gideon account is central to the unraveling action of Judges, for it functions as a pivot. Particularly important is the turning point of this pivot: Gideon's act of worship. What became clear is that Gideon's worship is impure. It is not based entirely on Yahwism. Gideon's actions in the latter part of the narrative reveal his impure belief: he acts brutally toward his own countrymen, constructs an ephod and leads idolatrous worship, and engages in liaisons with a foreign concubine. Perhaps most telling is the new dynamic arising with Gideon and continuing throughout the rest of the book: corruption in the judge himself. Before Gideon, it was the people who went astray, not the judges. However, Gideon introduces the reader to what happens when judges go astray: the nation unravels.

Puzzling Portraits

Therefore, to understand the Gideon account ethically, one must identify Gideon's vices and discern their role within the story and the larger book. Because Gideon's account is pivotal to all of Judges, his vices also should be understood in how they influence major dramatic movements, such as the shift to idolatry and apostasy. In what ways do Gideon's failings foreshadow the unraveling of all Israel? Before this study seeks to answer these questions, it is necessary to discuss the nature of vice.

VIRTUE AND VICE

Of primary importance is the relationship of virtue to vice. It may seem that vice is simply the opposite of virtue. Since a virtue is a character trait or disposition enabling someone to live the good life, vice must be a trait impairing or corroding it. Though this notion is basically true, there are important nuances. Fundamental to understanding these nuances is a better understanding of the nature of virtue.

Not every trait contributing to the good life is a virtue. Other positive qualities exist that are not virtues. Examples include bodily characteristics, such as health and strength, mental abilities, such as memory and concentration, and even skills of trades, such as those a good artisan may possess. What is the difference between these traits and actual virtues? Traditionally, the answer has been that virtues uniquely belong to the will, whereas these others do not.[2] Virtues are governed and guided by aspects of the will, particularly intention, desire, and attitude.[3] They are also evaluated according to these elements. Generosity, for example, is only a virtue if these elements align rightly. One would not consider a man generous if he gave to an orphanage for the wrong reasons, say for tax evasion or to bolster his public image. The particular significance of this concept for narrative ethics is that it helps discern difficult situations, when a seemingly *virtuous action* has occurred out of the *wrong motivation*.

2. Foot, *Virtues*, 4.
3. Ibid., 4–5.

A second quality of virtue is that it is corrective.[4] That is, virtue is a disposition that works to correct the temptation to go to one extreme or the other. Often an individual virtue stands in the middle of two extremes, two vices. For example, temperance stands between hedonism and asceticism. It is not, then, simply that virtues correct tendencies, but that they hold one in the proper balance between extremes. In addition to keeping certain excessive tendencies in check, virtues may also serve to guard against lack of motivation.[5] The virtuous person does not just avoid behaving poorly, but acts rightly, too. So it is that virtue stands in various ways as a corrective to poor dispositions and behaviors present in the human person.

Because virtue is both corrective and is necessarily related to the will, one may assume that the presence of vice is due to the corruption of one or both of these areas.[6] That is, if vice exists, it is because at least one of these elements is impure or absent. Therefore, the central question to ask is this: What are the specific deficiencies? This is important because it identifies particular workings within the human person that create vice and, in turn, it reveals what consequences certain vices have in life.

GIDEON AND THE GOOD LIFE

This section aims to explain Gideon's failure both to live the good life and to foster an environment for the good life for Israel. By discussing Gideon's central vices, it will be shown how each vice is a corruption of a virtue, and that each corrodes the possibility of living the good life. Also, the vices will be discussed as they relate to the larger plotline and themes of Gideon's account and the book of Judges. What is clear is that Gideon's own actions destroy the

---

4. Ibid., 8.
5. Ibid., 9.
6. For a technical discussion of vice, see "Degrees of Virtue and Vice" and "Varieties of Virtue and Vice," in Hurka, *Virtue*, 58–128. For a helpful discussion on the nuances of virtues, see Kruschwitz and Roberts, *Virtues*.

Puzzling Portraits

possibility of having a life of blessing (good harvests and progeny), peace, and the presence of God.

Courage

Courage is the virtue against which are set two of Gideon's vices: fear and brutality. Each errs to one side or the other of courage and, accordingly, uniquely affects the pursuit of the good life. Fear results in an inability to trust and believe God, thereby affecting one's experience of God's presence. Brutality generates tribal conflict, which impairs the attainment of peace. Therefore, in each instance the way in which Gideon failed to have courage is important to the corruption of the good life.

Gideon's fear is probably the clearest motif in the whole account. Time and again it is emphasized (6:11, 27, 36-40). But the question that arises regards its relation to the virtue of courage. If courage was the ideal, then how did Gideon fail by being fearful? Specifically, how is fear the corruption of courage? In the biblical sense, fear is the improper amount of self-concern. One fears because one cares too much for one's own well-being.[7] Often the effects of this vice are shown in relation to the plans of God and the larger community. That is, fear corrupts the execution of God's plan for the greater good. At this point it may be said that fear is at times, in the right proportion, a natural response. Nevertheless, the Gideon account goes to great lengths to show that this is not such a case.

---

7. In very general terms, fear in the Old Testament may be divided into two categories: godly and worldly fear. The former is a response to the divine and is viewed as appropriate and righteous behavior (Prov 1:7). The latter is a reaction to things of the world (weather, people, animals, etc.); it can carry both positive and negative connotations. Humans have an inborn sense of fear that at times is proper and fills a practical role: self-preservation. It is, for example, natural for someone to fear a lion (Amos 3:8). But when worldly fear grows to unhealthy levels, it is deemed problematic. Often, fear is seen as unhealthy when it stands in contrast to God's promises (Num 14:9-12). For a summary of the notion of fear in the Bible, see Terrien, "Fear."

The Ethics of Judges 7:15—8:33

At the beginning, the reader is introduced to the man Gideon in a time of great oppression. It seems sensible that, upon meeting the angel, Gideon asks why God's activity has not been present among his people (6:1–6). At this point in the story, fear seems like a natural response. However, the remaining scenes will eliminate this possibility. That fear is a vice becomes especially noticeable in the fleece testings (6:36–40). Though God clearly communicates his will to Gideon and accompanies this with signs, Gideon continues to fear. Here it can be seen that in Judges the vice of fear is associated with doubt or unbelief.[8] Thus fear is not just the improper amount of self-concern, but it is also the improper amount of concern for God. Fear disrupts the places of priority for self and for master. Of course, while Gideon is waffling with fear, the people are continuing under the oppression of Midian. In the case of a leader, the vice of fear does not just affect the individual, but also the community.[9]

When Gideon worships, however, his fear disappears and he is characterized by boldness. But a question arises: Why should one call this "boldness" and not "courage"? Earlier it was discussed that virtue may be thought of as a mean between two extremes. On either end lies a vice, a certain corruption of the virtue. Fear is a corruption of courage in that it places too much weight on self-concern. Its opposite is total recklessness, in which a person has no regard whatsoever for well-being. It is not suggested that Gideon's boldness is of this sort, but that it does corrupt elements of courage. Whereas his fear tended toward one end of the spectrum, his boldness tends toward the other. Neither is properly balanced enough to be called courage. In particular, his boldness is brutal and merciless (8:16–17, 21). Brutality, then, is a corruption of courage.

What also ensures that this boldness is not truly courage is the corruption of the will. It is not enough for a man like Gideon to have virtue-like behavior, for he must also have virtuous attitudes and motivations. If he does not have these, then an action cannot be considered virtuous, at least not entirely. Gideon's behavior

---

8. See Klein, *Triumph*, 59–60.
9. Younger, *Judges*, 182.

is somewhat akin to courage. He faces the Midianite army with only three hundred men, and tirelessly pursues and executes the princes and kings of Midian. However, throughout the account the narrator introduces a gamut of either questionable or clearly poor motivations. During the confrontation with Midian, Gideon has the people cry, "For the Lord and for Gideon!" (7:18). This, though the Lord has emphasized the people tend toward giving fellow humans credit instead of their God (7:2). So it is at least suspect as to why Gideon faces the Midianites: Was it for the Lord or for himself? A clearer case is Gideon's capture and execution of the Midianite kings, as vengeance for their killing of his brothers (8:19). Until now the reader had been led to believe that Gideon was pursuing these kings for the Lord's purposes. But here one learns it is merely for the quenching of Gideon's own revenge. Ultimately, Gideon's boldness is laced with too many corruptions of the will to be called courage. It is a vice that distorts his behavior.

Eloquence

Eloquence as a virtue in the Bible is important in that it brings about good (Gen 44:18–34; 41:25–37). The corruption of eloquence consequently causes harm. That is the case with Gideon. Language abuse causes tempers to flare and violence to occur. An ineloquent use of speech by Gideon corrupts the good life by initiating strife. It destroys the possibility of achieving the goal of peaceful living.

The virtue of eloquence may seem trite compared to others, such as courage, justice, or mercy. But the fact is that eloquence, too, is an important element of the good life. This is especially the case in biblical narrative, which places a high value on the spoken word. In particular, the area of the good life most often affected by eloquence is peaceful living (Prov 15:1). A world so full of conflict is bound to need cogent resolution. Eloquence is generally understood as the ability to speak clearly and persuasively about an issue. However, it should be noted that eloquence aligns with what is right and true (Prov 14:5). That is, speech is not considered

The Ethics of Judges 7:15—8:33

eloquent if used to fool or bring about unrighteous ends. Therefore, eloquence is no trite virtue. It can create enlightenment and motivation and can resolve conflict.

Eloquence as a virtue is most notable in Gideon's encounter with the Ephraimites. For whatever reason, the men of Ephraim were very angry with Gideon for not inviting them to take part in the battle (8:1). Gideon, however, skillfully addresses the situation and diffuses their hostility (8:2–3). Already it has been argued that this scene depicts the tribal tensions of the time and also the combative nature of the Ephraimites; it also demonstrates how the virtue of eloquence could be exercised to resolve some of these issues. However, it is equally true that the opposite of eloquence, harsh and course language, can be divisive. This is what is shown in the following scene. Immediately following this display of eloquence, Gideon clashes with the leaders of Succoth and Peniel (8:4–8, 13–17). They did treat him disrespectfully, but not badly enough to warrant Gideon's reaction. Yet he killed the men and destroyed their towns. It is here for the first time in Judges that a judge turns the sword on his own people, a trend that will worsen. Therefore, an absence of eloquence, manifested in harsh words, leads to tribal conflict. Tribal conflict is an obvious failure to live out peace, an element of the good life.

Justice

The virtue of justice may be paired with the vice of injustice. There are a host of ways in which justice may be corrupted into injustice. In the Gideon account, the corruption is not always obvious. It takes the form of excess judgment or improper motive. Both Israelites and non-Israelites are the object of Gideon's injustice. With the Israelites, Gideon's behavior corrupts the good life in that it causes tribal conflict. It thus corrupts peaceful living. However, with the non-Israelites, Gideon's actions cannot be said to disrupt tribal unity. Instead, his actions must be understood as the failure to imitate God.

Justice may be understood as the giving of just ends, such as when the vulnerable are treated fairly and the unjust judged. As

Puzzling Portraits

with other virtues, justice may involve other elements and qualifications. Of particular interest to this study is the notion of just punishment, the idea that the violator gets neither too minor nor too harsh a punishment, but one that is fitting. Within the Gideon story there are two poignant instances to which this principle lends itself, and each time Gideon doles out too harsh a punishment. It is somewhat ironic that in his very acts of "justice" Gideon is exercising the vice of injustice.

Gideon's punishment of the leaders of Succoth and Peniel was unjust in that it was too harsh and done out of improper motive. Indeed, he had been wronged, but for Gideon to beat some men, kill others, and raze the towns (8:16–17) was certainly too harsh. Additionally, it was suggested earlier that Gideon was motivated by rage at the leaders' doubts of his character. However, to have one's personal ability doubted is no reason for rage, and rage is no motivation for exercising judgment. Gideon is therefore in the wrong concerning motive. The effect of Gideon's harsh punishments and unacceptable motive is tribal disunity, which is a corruption of the peaceful living element of the good life.

The execution of Zebah and Zalmunna, kings of Midian, also reveals the vice of injustice. It may appear that Gideon's execution of the kings was legitimate, since they did deserve to be put to death. But the problem is that Gideon's motive was wrong. An emphasis of the execution scene (8:15–21) is Gideon's reason for pursuing the kings: a personal vendetta. This revelation comes as a surprise, for the reader had been led to believe Gideon had acted according to Yahweh's will. One might argue that, even with wrong motive, Gideon apparently brought peace to the land (8:28). Can it not be said that Gideon did in fact accomplish an element of the good life? No, it cannot. This invokes the classic phrase, "The ends do not justify the means." Overarching the whole enterprise of Old Testament ethics is the imitation of God.[10] Actions cannot be evaluated simply by their results; they also must be compared to the character of God. The reason Gideon's actions fail is because they are unjust. God, however, is characterized by holiness and justice,

10. Wenham, *Story*, 104–7.

The Ethics of Judges 7:15—8:33

even as he relates to non-Israelites (Exod 23:9; Ps 9:8). Gideon's vice of injustice creates a corruption of the good life and leads to tribal disunity and the non-imitation of God.

Piety

It was argued that the presence of God, an important indicator of the good life, is eerily absent from the latter half of the Gideon account. This was attributed to Gideon's impure belief, which is manifested in his increasingly immoral tendencies. Gideon also was stubbornly disobedient. The combined portrait suggests a failure in Gideon concerning the central virtue of piety. Three particular examples are of interest—Gideon's kingship, the making of an ephod, and the foreign liaison. Each has unique and lasting implications for the good life.

Piety, as Wenham defines it, involves obedience and reverence for God and a certain devoutness of life.[11] It is the right attitudes, dispositions, and behaviors necessary to be in proper relationship with God. It can be assumed that the corruption of piety stems from compromises in these areas. The last chapter concluded that the book of Judges' ideal was for Yahweh, not a human, to be king over Israel. Gideon's own words reflect his knowledge of this fact (8:23). However, it also was noted that, though Gideon denounced the offer to be king, his life took on kingly prerogatives. There is evidence that Gideon did live in a kingly manner, which highlights his disobedience to God's will.

Kingship was not considered ideal for Israel because it tended to corrupt the intensions for Yahweh's society. Chief of these intentions was Torah rule. If Israel were not governed by Torah and Yahweh, it most certainly would go astray. That is precisely what happened with Gideon. From the point at which Gideon apparently began to live a kingly life, Israel only declined in regard to its connection with Torah and Yahweh. The details of this decline have been discussed already. The point here is that Gideon's

11. Ibid., 89.

impiety contributed to the corruption of the good life. Through his own impiety Gideon led all Israel astray.

One particular manifestation of the move away from Torah rule is Gideon's construction of an ephod. The text says that the ephod caused Gideon, his family, and all Israel to go astray (8:27). What is interesting about the ephod incident is that it reveals the nature of idolatry. The Torah was not omitted suddenly from Israelite life; it was replaced slowly. An originally legitimate cultic item, the ephod, was tweaked and used in a new way. Perhaps it resembled current Canaanite practices. Whatever the case, it seems the ephod worship was viewed as reasonable practice by the Israelites. By Gideon's impiety, Israel was led away from Torah rule and into idolatry. This damaged the possibility of the good life in that it negated the presence of God.

Gideon's impiety is demonstrated also in his harem. The damage wrought on the good life by Gideon's establishment of a harem touches three main areas: progeny, peace, and the presence of God. Each problem is rooted in Abimelech, the son of a Shechemite concubine with whom Gideon had sinful sexual relations. Gideon is said to have had seventy sons from many wives (8:30). Though it might be argued that the phrase "many wives" stands in condemnation of Gideon's harem, his seventy sons could be seen as a blessing, a sign of the good life. The problem is that Gideon's sin spoils the fruit of his good life. In 9:5 the narrator records that Abimelech kills all of Gideon's sons, save one (Jotham). The narrative implicitly shows that the result of Gideon's impiety, Abimelech, destroys an element of the good life, progeny. Abimelech's life also destroys the possibility of another element of the good life, peace. Strife and carnage characterize Abimelech's existence. In addition to the slaughter of Gideon's sons, the Abimelech story also records the ongoing fight between Abimelech and the Shechemites (9:23–54). There is constant war in the land. It is brought to an end with Abimelech's death (9:55), which is a direct judgment of God (9:56). What is clear is that the very life of Abimelech made it impossible for peace to exist in the land. Gideon's impiety, which gave rise to Abimelech, is shown to be the cause of a lack of peace in Israel.

The Ethics of Judges 7:15—8:33

The presence of God, too, was corrupted by Abimelech. It was noted that the latter half of the Gideon story betrays an eerie absence of Yahweh. Abimelech's account shares this characteristic. The way in which it is manifested is somewhat different, though. Peculiar to Abimelech's story is the absolute absence of the name "Yahweh." Even "Elohim" is used very little, usually only to say that God judged Abimelech (9:23-24, 56). Further, Abimelech is never portrayed in relationship with God or seeking his will. God is only the distant and sovereign judge, not a caretaker of people. The impression, then, is that Abimelech has done nothing to foster the presence of God in the land and, in fact, has only driven it away. It may be assumed that Gideon's vice of impiety, which led to Abimelech, has caused further damage to the good life by estranging Israel from her God.

CONCLUSIONS

This chapter analyzed the ethics of Judges 7:15—8:33. It was suggested that due to the negative nature of the book of Judges, it is best to extract Gideon's vices and contrast them with the virtues of the ideal-person identikit (as constructed by Wenham). In order to properly understand the role of vice in the ethical life, a discussion of the relationship between virtue and vice was engaged in. It was demonstrated that vice is the corruption of virtue. If virtue is seen as the mean between two extremes, then vice (often) is an error to one or the other of those poles. This is valuable to ethical inquiry, because it illumines exactly how virtues are corrupted and how their corruption affects the moral life. The final section analyzed Gideon's particular vices and showed how they corroded the various elements of the good life: blessing (good harvests and progeny), peace, and the presence of God. The chapter concluded with the notion that Gideon's behavior led both himself and the nation into a state without blessing, peace, or God's presence.

7

Conclusions

SUMMARY

The goal of this study was to explore the ways in which character study might aid the ethical interpretation of complex characters. It was found that characterization is helpful in that it illumines the subtle and nuanced details concerning characters. Chief is characterization's ability to reveal the inner attitudes and dispositions of actors. The inner beings of characters are vitally important to ethics, for they complete the story for which action is but a conclusion. That is, to know one's inner being is to know the whole gamut of elements that gave rise to one's behavior. The revelation of the inner dispositions helps the interpreter more fully understand a text's ethics.

Chapter 1 sketched the field of Old Testament ethics in order to show the need for a better understanding of narrative ethics. Views of four scholars were summarized and briefly discussed: Walter Kaiser, John Rogerson, Christopher Wright, and Waldemar Janzen. Wright and Janzen's views were most helpful of the four,

Conclusions

though not entirely satisfactory. In particular, it was argued that a fuller understanding was needed concerning the place of narrative in general and the role of individual stories specifically.

Chapter 2 approached these issues using the work of Robin Parry and Gordon Wenham as guides. Parry's basic contention is that narrative is both essential to Old Testament ethics and offers it a unique contribution. To demonstrate that narrative is essential, Parry uses the ethical models of John Barton: imitation of God, natural law, and obedience to the declared will of God. Parry shows each model's dependence on narrative; without narrative, each model would unravel. An idea of Wenham serves as the base for Parry's discussion on narrative's unique contribution to Old Testament ethics. Wenham forwards the unique idea that, contra common opinion, narrative (not law) is the reservoir of Old Testament ideals. Law simply serves as the cutoff point at which behavior becomes morally impermissible and punishable. Narrative reveals the ideal existence, the kind of life people are supposed to live. Thus for ethics, law is the basement and narrative the ceiling

Chapter 3 discussed methods by which to interpret the ethics of individual stories. Wenham and Parry were again used. Wenham suggested three elements basic to understanding individual stories: virtue ethics, virtue criteria, and rhetorical criticism. Virtue ethics is an ethical system especially attuned to reading narrative. It seeks to understand particular virtues and their ultimate goal, the incarnation of "the good" in the good life. Wenham's intent is to discern commended virtues from individual stories and to identify their end. Wenham's second element, virtue criteria, was a set of criteria meant to ensure the validity of virtues within a text. Rhetorical criticism was the third element. Its purpose is to lay bare the particular ideas of the author by understanding the way in which the book was shaped and organized. It takes into account the many features of composition that direct readers to meaning. Parry offered a specific rhetorical method. Though quite helpful, it was suggested that Parry's approach would benefit from the additional tools of theme and characterization.

Chapter 4 discussed the value of theme and characterization for interpreting complex characters ethically. It was suggested that theme helped solve one of the major problems with complex characters: conflicting signals. Theme establishes a center point, a common thread for the many parts of a story. It allows readers to understand story messages by relating rhetorical elements one to another. Characterization helped solve another problem with complex characters: difficult details. A knowledge of the portrayal of biblical characters allows the reader to discern the presence and significance of subtle details. Further, characterization illumines the inner being of characters, which is important to ethics.

Chapter 5 presented an exegetical analysis of Judges 7:15—8:33. The works of Robert O'Connell and Yairah Amit served as good guides for the discussion of the book of Judges. Their ideas were tempered with those of other scholars. It was found that, contra O'Connell and Amit, the primary purpose of Judges is not to argue for kingship. Instead, the book aims to call Israel back unto covenant faithfulness by showing the horrors of disobedience in the period of the judges. Gideon's story is a pivot in the book. He is the first judge to engage in covenant infidelity. Gideon's sin of idolatry, tribal brutality, and foreign liaisons lead him and Israel down a descending moral path. After him, the judges and the nation will only grow increasingly worse.

Chapter 6 applied the cumulative findings of theory and exegesis to an ethical reading of Judges 7:15—8:33. It was suggested that a similar strategy to more positive narratives be employed, except to extract vice in place of virtue. Because vice is a corruption of virtue, one may use it to discern the nature of virtue's corruption and its ill effects on the good life. Gideon's life was mined for vices, and each vice was analyzed in relation to its impact on the Old Testament idea of the good life. It was shown precisely how and why Gideon failed morally, and what consequences it had on him personally and also the nation.

Conclusions

IMPLICATIONS

There is much work to be done in interpreting complex characters, as most scholarship has only touched on the issue in ancillary ways. Perhaps the two main reasons for the lack of attention to difficult characters are the opposing poles of biblical scholarship: critical and dogmatic-conservative. The former holds that contrasting elements in individual characters are a result of redaction. There is, then, very little motivation to look for coherent meaning. The latter often denies the existence of difficult features, preferring instead to settle on one simple and straightforward meaning. Either way, it is clear that to understand complex characters readers must adopt a more sophisticated approach.

Perhaps two fields that would contribute greatly to the understanding of complex characters in narrative ethics are literary theory and theological anthropology. Literary theory, as shown in this study, holds much promise for the discernment of particular character behaviors and their motivations. However, more work needs to be done concerning how literary theory may be employed to illumine the biblical text. Theological anthropology is necessary to the task for a couple of reasons. First, there is a need to better understand the biblical view of the human person. Virtue ethics in particular depends on the concept of humanity, for this determines "the good." That which a person should strive toward depends on what an individual is meant to be. Concerning the issue of the good, this study has followed the work of Gordon Wenham. However, it is recognized that what is needed for a better grasp of the good is a deeper and more nuanced examination of the biblical theology of the human person. Second, theological anthropology might clarify the nature of particular complex characters. At what level is a character meant to be interpreted, and at what level is it meant to reflect the larger human condition? For this question, Robert Alter and Meir Sternberg have been consulted for this study. However, there remain many unturned stones in other areas.

Bibliography

Alter, Robert. *The Art of Biblical Narrative*. New York: Basic Books, 1981.
———. *The David Story: A Translation with Commentary of 1 and 2 Samuel*. New York: W. W. Norton, 1999.
Amit, Yairah. *The Book of Judges: The Art of Editing*. Translated by Jonathan Chipman. Leiden: Brill, 1999.
———. "The Multi-Purpose 'Leading Word' and the Problems of Its Usage." *Prooftexts* 9 (January 1989) 99–114.
———. *Reading Biblical Narratives: Literary Criticism and the Hebrew Bible*. Minneapolis: Fortress, 2001.
Arnold, Bill T. *1 & 2 Samuel*. New International Version Application Commentary. Grand Rapids: Zondervan, 2003.
Assis, Elie. *Self-Interest or Communal Interest: An Ideology of Leadership in the Gideon, Abimelech and Jephthah Narratives (Judg 6–12)*. Supplements to Vetus Testamentum 106. Leiden, The Netherlands: Brill, 2006.
Auerbach, Erich. "Odysseus' Scar." In *Mimesis: The Representation of Reality in Western Literature*, 3–23. Translated by Willard R. Trask. Princeton: Princeton University Press, 1953.
Auld, A. Graeme. "Gideon: Hacking at the Heart of the Old Testament." *Vetus Testamentum* 39, no. 3 (July 1989) 257–67.
Bar-Efrat, Shimon. *Narrative Art in the Bible*. London: T & T Clark, 2004.
———. "Some Observations on the Analysis of Structure in Biblical Narrative." In *Beyond Form Criticism: Essays in Old Testament Literary Criticism*, edited by Paul R. House, 186–205. Sources for Biblical and Theological Study 2. Winona Lake, IN: Eisenbrauns, 1992.
Bartholomew, Craig, Colin Greene, and Karl Möller, eds. *After Pentecost: Language and Biblical Interpretation*. Scripture and Hermeneutics 2. Grand Rapids: Zondervan, 2001.
Bartholomew, Craig, and Michael W. Goheen. *The Drama of Scripture: Finding Our Place in the Biblical Story*. Grand Rapids: Baker, 2004.
Barton, John. "The Basis of Ethics in the Hebrew Bible." *Semeia* 66 (1994) 11–22.

Bibliography

———. *Ethics and the Old Testament*. Harrisburg, PA: Trinity Press International, 1998.

———. "Understanding Old Testament Ethics." *Journal for the Study of the Old Testament* 9 (1978) 44–64.

———. *Understanding Old Testament Ethics: Approaches and Explorations*. Louisville, KY: Westminster John Knox, 2003.

Berlin, Adele. *Poetics and Interpretation of Biblical Narrative*. Winona Lake, IN: Eisenbrauns, 1994.

Birch, Bruce C. *Let Justice Roll Down: The Old Testament, Ethics, and Christian Life*. Louisville: Westminster John Knox, 1991.

———. "Moral Agency, Community, and the Character of God in the Hebrew Bible." *Semeia* 66 (1994) 23–41.

Birch, Bruce C., and Larry L. Rasmussen. *Bible and Ethics in the Christian Life*. Rev. ed. Minneapolis: Augsburg, 1989.

Block, Daniel I. *Judges, Ruth*. New American Commentary 6. Nashville: Broadman & Holman, 1999.

———. "The Period of the Judges: Religious Disintegration Under Tribal Rule." In *Israel's Apostasy and Restoration: Essays in Honor of Roland K. Harrison*, edited by Avraham Gileadi and R.K. Harrison, 39–57. Grand Rapids: Baker Book House, 1988.

———. "Will the Real Gideon Please Stand Up? Narrative Style and Intention in Judges 6–9." *Journal of the Evangelical Theological Society* 40, no. 3 (September 1997) 353–66.

Bluedorn, Wolfgang. *Yahweh versus Baalism: A Theological Reading of the Gideon-Abimelech Narrative*. Journal for the Study of the Old Testament Supplement Series 329. Sheffield, UK: Sheffield Academic, 2001.

Boling, Robert G. *Judges*. The Anchor Bible 6. Garden City, NY: Doubleday, 1975.

Booth, Wayne C. *The Company We Keep: An Ethics of Fiction*. Berkeley: University of California Press, 1988.

———. *The Rhetoric of Fiction*. Chicago: University of Chicago Press, 1983.

Bowman, Richard G. "The Complexity of Character and the Ethics of Complexity: The Case of King David." In *Character and Scripture: Moral Formation, Community, and Biblical Interpretation*, edited by William P. Brown, 73–97. Grand Rapids: Eerdmans, 2002.

———. "Narrative Criticism: Human Purpose in Conflict with Divine Presence." In *Judges and Method: New Approaches in Biblical Studies*, edited by Gale E. Yee, 17–44. Minneapolis: Fortress, 1995.

Brettler, Marc. "The Book of Judges: Literature as Politics." *Journal of Biblical Literature* 108, no. 3 (Fall 1989) 395–418.

Brown, William P., ed. *Character and Scripture: Moral Formation, Community, and Biblical Interpretation*. Grand Rapids: Eerdmans, 2002.

Brueggemann, Walter. *Theology of the Old Testament*. Minneapolis: Fortress, 1997.

Bibliography

Carmichael, Calum M. *The Spirit of Biblical Law*. Athens: University of Georgia Press, 1996.
Carroll R., M. Daniel. "Seeking the Virtues among the Prophets: The Book of Amos as a Test Case." *Ex Auditu* 17 (2001) 77-96.
Clines, David J. A. *The Theme of the Pentateuch*. Journal for the Study of the Old Testament Supplement Series 10. Sheffield, UK: Sheffield Academic, 1978.
Coles, Robert. *The Call of Stories: Teaching and the Moral Imagination*. Boston: Houghton Mifflin, 1989.
Craigie, Peter C. *The Book of Deuteronomy*. New International Commentary on the Old Testament. London: Hodder & Stoughton, 1976.
Cundall, Arthur E., and Leon Morris. *Judges and Ruth*. Tyndale Old Testament Commentaries 7. Downers Grove, IL: InterVarsity, 1968.
Damrosch, David. *The Narrative Covenant: Transformations of Genre in the Growth of Biblical Literature*. San Francisco: Harper & Row, 1987.
Davies, Gwynne Henton. "Judges 8:22-23." *Vetus Testamentum* 13 (April 1963) 151-57.
Dreytza, Manfred. "יד" and "כף." In *New International Dictionary of Old Testament Theology & Exegesis*, edited by Willem VanGemeren, 2:402-5 and 2:686-87. Grand Rapids: Zondervan, 1997.
Exum, Cheryl J. "The Centre Cannot Hold: Thematic and Textual Instabilities in Judges." *Catholic Biblical Quarterly* 52, no. 3 (July 1990) 410-29.
Fokkelman, J. P. *Reading Biblical Narrative: An Introductory Guide*. Translated by Ineke Smit. Tools for Biblical Studies Series 1. Leiden, The Netherlands: Deo, 1999.
Foot, Philippa. *Virtues and Vices and Other Essays in Moral Philosophy*. Berkeley: University of California Press, 1978.
Fretheim, Terence E. "חזה." In *New International Dictionary of Old Testament Theology and Exegesis*, edited by Willem VanGemeren, 2:42-44. Grand Rapids: Zondervan, 1997.
Garsiel, Moshe. "Homiletic Name-Derivations as a Literary Device in the Gideon Narrative: Judges 6-8." *Vetus Testamentum* 43, no. 3 (July 1993) 302-17.
Gerbrandt, Gerald E. *Kingship According to the Deuteronomistic History*. Society of Biblical Literature Dissertation Series 87. Atlanta: Scholars, 1986.
Good, Edwin M. *Irony in the Old Testament*. Sheffield, UK: Almond Press, 1981.
Gooding, D. W. "The Composition of the Book of Judges." *Eretz-Israel* 16 (1982) 70-79.
Gray, John. *Joshua, Judges, Ruth*. New Century Bible Commentary. Grand Rapids: Eerdmans, 1986.
Greenspahn, Frederick E. "The Theology of the Framework of Judges." *Vetus Testamentum* 36 (1986) 385-96.
Gros Louis, Kenneth R. R., James S. Ackerman, and Thayer S. Warshaw, eds. *Literary Interpretations of Biblical Narratives*. Bible in Literature Courses. Nashville: Abingdon, 1974.

Bibliography

Gunn, David M. "Joshua and Judges." In *The Literary Guide to the Bible*, edited by Robert Alter and Frank Kermode, 102–21. Cambridge, MA: Belknap Press of Harvard University Press, 1987.

———. *Judges*. Blackwell Bible Commentaries. Oxford: Blackwell, 2005.

———. "New Directions in the Study of Biblical Hebrew Narrative." In *Beyond Form Criticism: Essays in Old Testament Literary Criticism*, edited by Paul R. House, 412–22. Sources for Biblical and Theological Study 2. Winona Lake, IN: Eisenbrauns, 1992.

Gunn, David M., and Dana Nolan Fewell. *Narrative in the Hebrew Bible*. Oxford: Oxford University Press, 1993.

Hauerwas, Stanley. *A Community of Character: Toward a Constructive Christian Social Ethic*. Notre Dame, IN: University of Notre Dame Press, 1981.

Hauerwas, Stanley, and Charles Robert Pinches. *Christians Among the Virtues: Theological Conversations with Ancient and Modern Ethics*. Notre Dame, IN: University of Notre Dame Press, 1997.

Hauerwas, Stanley, and L. Gregory Jones, eds. *Why Narrative? Readings in Narrative Theology*. Grand Rapids: Eerdmans, 1989.

House, Paul. *Old Testament Theology*. Downers Grove, IL: InterVarsity, 1998.

Howard, David M., Jr. "The Case for Kingship in Deuteronomy and the Former Prophets." *Westminster Theological Journal* 52, no. 1 (1990) 101–15.

Hurka, Thomas. *Virtue, Vice, and Value*. Oxford: Oxford University Press, 2001.

Hursthouse, Rosalind. *On Virtue Ethics*. Oxford: Oxford University Press, 1999.

Janzen, J. Gerald. Review of *The Poetics of Biblical Narrative: Ideological Literature and the Drama of Reading*, by Meir Sternberg. *Theology Today* 44, no. 2 (July 1987) 285–86.

Janzen, Waldemar. *Old Testament Ethics: A Paradigmatic Approach*. Louisville: Westminster John Knox, 1994.

Jobes, Karen H., and Moisés Silva. *Invitation to the Septuagint*. Grand Rapids: Baker Academic, 2000.

Kaiser, Walter C. "A Comparison of the Principlized and Paradigmatic Approaches to Biblical Law." Paper presented to the Evangelical Theological Society, Philadelphia, November 2005.

———. *Toward Old Testament Ethics*. Grand Rapids: Zondervan, 1983.

———. *Toward Rediscovering the Old Testament*. Grand Rapids: Zondervan, 1987.

Klein, Lillian R. *The Triumph of Irony in the Book of Judges*. Journal for the Study of the Old Testament Supplement Series 68. Sheffield, UK: Almond Press, 1988.

Knight, Douglas A. "Introduction: Ethics, Ancient Israel, and the Hebrew Bible." *Semeia* 66 (1994) 1–8.

Kruschwitz, Robert B., and Robert C. Roberts. *The Virtues: Contemporary Essays on Moral Character*. Belmont, CA: Wadsworth, 1987.

Kuhn, Thomas S. *Structure of Scientific Revolutions*. Chicago: University of Chicago Press, 1962.

Bibliography

Lee, Bernon. "Fragmentation of Reader Focus in the Preamble to Battle in Judges 6.1–7.14." *Journal for the Study of the Old Testament* 97, no. 3 (March 2002) 65–86.

Lewis, Theodore. "The Identity and Function of El/Baal Berith." *Journal of Biblical Literature* 115, no. 3 (Fall 1996) 401–23.

Licht, Jacob. *Storytelling in the Bible*. Jerusalem: Magnes Press, 1978.

Long, V. Philips, ed. *Israel's Past in Present Research: Essays on Ancient Israelite Historiography*. Sources for Biblical and Theological Study 7. Winona Lake, IN: Eisenbrauns, 1999.

Longman, Tremper, III. *Literary Approaches to Biblical Interpretation*. Foundations of Contemporary Interpretation 3. Grand Rapids: Academic, 1987.

MacIntyre, Alasdair C. *After Virtue: A Study in Moral Theory*. Notre Dame, IN: University of Notre Dame Press, 1981.

McConville, J. Gordon. *Deuteronomy*. Apollos Old Testament Commentary 5. Leicester, UK: Apollos, 2002.

———. "Law and Monarchy in the Old Testament." In *A Royal Priesthood? The Use of the Bible Ethically and Politically: A Dialogue with Oliver O'Donovan*. Scripture and Hermeneutic 3, edited by Craig Bartholomew, Jonathan Chaplin, Robert Song, and Al Wolters, 69–88. Grand Rapids: Zondervan, 2002.

Mendenhall, George E. *The Tenth Generation: The Origins of Biblical Tradition*. Baltimore: Johns Hopkins University Press, 1973.

Merrill, Eugene H. *Deuteronomy*. New American Commentary 4. Nashville: Broadman & Holman, 1994.

Meyers, Carol. "Ephod." In *The Anchor Bible Dictionary*, edited by David Noel Freedman, 2:550. New York: Doubleday, 1992.

Meynet, Roland. *Rhetorical Analysis: An Introduction to Biblical Rhetoric*. Journal for the Study of the Old Testament Supplement Series 256. Sheffield, UK: Sheffield Academic, 1998.

Moberly, R. W. L. *Genesis 12–50*. Old Testament Guides 2. Sheffield, UK: Sheffield Academic, 1992.

———. *The Old Testament of the Old Testament: Patriarchal Narratives and Mosaic Yahwism*. Minneapolis: Fortress, 1992.

Moore, George Foot. *A Critical and Exegetical Commentary on Judges*. International Critical Commentary on the Holy Scriptures of the Old and New Testaments 7. New York: Scribner, 1895.

Noth, Martin. *The Deuteronomistic History*. Translated by Jane Doull. Journal for the Study of the Old Testament Supplement Series 15. Sheffield, UK: Sheffield Academic, 1981.

Nussbaum, Martha C. *Love's Knowledge: Essays on Philosophy and Literature*. New York: Oxford University Press, 1990.

———. *Poetic Justice: The Literary Imagination and the Public Life*. Boston: Beacon, 1995.

Bibliography

O'Connell, Robert H. *The Rhetoric of the Book of Judges*. Supplements to Vetus Testamentum 63. Leiden, The Netherlands: Brill, 1996.

Parry, Robin A. "Greeks Bearing Gifts? Appropriating Nussbaum (Appropriating Aristotle) for a Christian Approach to Old Testament Narrative Ethics." *European Journal of Theology* 9, no. 1 (2000) 61–73.

———. *Old Testament Story and Christian Ethics: The Rape of Dinah as a Case Study*. Wayneboro, GA: Paternoster, 2004.

Pleins, J. David. *The Social Visions of the Hebrew Bible: A Theological Introduction*. Louisville: Westminster John Knox, 2001.

Polzin, Robert. *Moses and the Deuteronomist: Deuteronomy, Joshua, Judges*. A Literary Study of the Deuteronomic History 1. New York: Seabury, 1980.

Preuss, H. D. "חוה." In *Theological Dictionary of the Old Testament*, edited by G. Johannes Botterweck and Helmer Ringgren, translated by David E. Green, 4:248–56. Grand Rapids: Eerdmans, 1977.

Provan, Iain, V. Philips Long, and Tremper Longman III. *A Biblical History of Israel*. Louisville: Westminster John Knox, 2003.

Rabin, Chaim. "The Origin of the Hebrew Word Pīlegeš." *Journal of Jewish Studies* 25, no. 3 (Winter 1974) 353–64.

Richter, Sandra L. "Deuteronomistic History." In *Dictionary of the Old Testament: Historical Books*, edited by Bill T. Arnold and H. G. M. Williamson, 219–30. Downers Grove, IL: InterVarsity, 2005.

Ricouer, Paul. *Oneself as Another*. Translated by Kathleen Blamey. Chicago: University of Chicago Press, 1992.

Roberts, Robert C. "Kierkegaard, Wittgenstein, and a Method of 'Virtue Ethics.'" In *Kierkegaard in Post/Modernity*, edited by Martin J. Matuštík and Merold Westphal, 142–66. Bloomington: Indiana University Press, 1995.

Rodd, Cyril S. *Glimpses of a Strange Land: Studies in Old Testament Ethics*. Edinburgh: T & T Clark, 2001.

Rogerson, John W. *Theory and Practice in Old Testament Ethics*. Edited by M. Daniel Carroll R. Journal for the Study of the Old Testament Supplement Series 405. New York: T & T Clark, 2004.

Rogerson, John W., Margaret Davies, and M. Daniel Carroll R, eds. *The Bible in Ethics: The Second Sheffield Colloquium*. Journal for the Study of the Old Testament Supplement Series 207. Sheffield, UK: Sheffield Academic, 1995.

Ryken, Leland. *How to Read the Bible as Literature*. Grand Rapids: Academie, 1984.

———. *The Literature of the Bible*. Grand Rapids: Zondervan, 1976.

———. *Words of Delight: A Literary Introduction to the Bible*. Grand Rapids: Baker, 1987.

Sage, Victor. "Theme." In *A Dictionary of Modern Critical Terms*, edited by Roger Fowler, 248. London: Routledge, 1990.

Schneider, Tammi J. *Judges*. Berit Olam: Studies in Hebrew Narrative & Poetry. Collegeville, MN: Liturgical Press, 2000.

Bibliography

Seely, Jo Ann H. "Succoth." In *The Anchor Bible Dictionary*, edited by David Noel Freedman, 6:217-18. New York: Doubleday, 1992.

Segal, Naomi. Review of *The Poetics of Biblical Narrative: Ideological Literature and the Drama of Reading*, by Meir Sternberg. *Vetus Testamentum* 38 (April 1988): 243-49.

Slayton, Joel. "Penuel." In *The Anchor Bible Dictionary*, edited by David Noel Freedman, 5:223. New York: Doubleday, 1992.

Soggin, J. Alberto. *Judges: A Commentary*. Translated by John Bowden. Old Testament Library. Philadelphia: Westminster, 1982.

Sternberg, Meir. *The Poetics of Biblical Narrative: Ideological Literature and the Drama of Reading*. Bloomington: Indiana University Press, 1985.

Tanner, J Paul. "The Gideon Narrative as the Focal Point of Judges." *Bibliotheca Sacra* 149 (April-June 1992) 146-61.

Terrien, Samuel. "Fear." In *The Interpreter's Dictionary of the Bible*, edited by George Arthur Buttrick, 2:256-60. Nashville: Abingdon, 1962.

Toombs, Lawrence E. "Shechem (Place)." In *The Anchor Bible Dictionary*, edited by David Noel Freedman, 5:1174-86. New York: Doubleday, 1992.

Trible, Phyllis. *Rhetorical Criticism: Context, Method, and the Book of Jonah*. Minneapolis: Fortress, 1994.

Walton, John H. "A New Equation: (Narrative + Law) x Covenant = Torah." Unpublished paper presented at the Evangelical Theological Society in Toronto, November 2002.

Webb, Barry G. *The Book of Judges: An Integrated Reading*. Journal for the Study of the Old Testament Supplement Series 46. Sheffield, UK: Journal for the Study of the Old Testament Press, 1987.

Wenham, Gordon J. "The Gap between Law and Ethics in the Bible." *Journal of Jewish Studies* 48, no. 1 (Spring 1997) 17-29.

———. *Story as Torah: Reading the Old Testament Ethically*. Edinburgh: T & T Clark, 2000.

Wilcock, Michael. *The Message of Judges: Grace Abounding*. The Bible Speaks Today. Downers Grove, IL: InterVarsity, 1992.

Williams, Jay G. "The Structure of Judges 2:6-16:13." *Journal for the Study of the Old Testament* 49 (February 1977) 77-86.

Wright, Christopher J. H. "Ethics." In *Dictionary of the Old Testament: Historical Books*, edited by Bill T. Arnold and H. G. M. Williamson, 259-68. Downers Grove, IL: InterVarsity, 2005.

———. *Old Testament Ethics for the People of God*. Downers Grove, IL: InterVarsity, 2004.

Younger, K. Lawson, Jr. "Judges 1 in Its Near Eastern Literary Context." In *Faith, Tradition, and History: Old Testament Historiography in Its Ancient Near Eastern Context*, edited by A. R. Millard, James K. Hoffmeier, and David W. Baker. Winona Lake, IN: Eisenbrauns, 1994.

———. *Judges and Ruth*. New International Version Application Commentary. Grand Rapids: Zondervan, 2002.

www.ingramcontent.com/pod-product-compliance
Lightning Source LLC
Chambersburg PA
CBHW072152160426
43197CB00012B/2356